THE POWDER OF
SYMPATHY

THE POWDER OF SYMPATHY

BY
CHRISTOPHER MORLEY

Strange, when you come to think of it, that of all the countless folk who have lived before our time on this planet not one is known in history or in legend as having died of laughter.
—MAX BEERBOHM

ILLUSTRATED
BY
WALTER JACK DUNCAN

S. B. GUNDY   TORONTO
DOUBLEDAY, PAGE & COMPANY
GARDEN CITY   NEW YORK
1923

DEDICATION

TO FELIX RIESENBERG and FRANKLIN ABBOTT

DEAR FELIX, DEAR FRANK:—It is a pleasant circumstance that as one sets about collecting material for a book, scissoring night after night among scrapbooks to determine what may or may not be worth revisiting the glimpses of the press, there comes to mind with perfect naturalness who should carry the onus of the dedication. For a book is a frail and human emanation, and has its own instinctive disposition toward a certain kind of people. These Powders of Sympathy I hopefully sprinkle in your direction.

Another good friend warned me seriously, some time ago, against the danger of being too apologetic in a preface. For, said he, people always read prefaces and dedications, even if nought else; if you deprecate, you at once persuade them to the same attitude. And

Dedication

to you two, of all readers, I need not explain just how
these pieces were written, day by day, out of the pres-
sure and hilarity and contention of the mind. I
have made no attempt to conceal their ephemeral ori-
gin. They were almost all written for a newspaper, and
contain many references to journalism. And, if I
may speak my inmost heart, I have had a sincere hope
that they might, in collected form, play some small
part in encouraging the youngest generation of jour-
nalists to be themselves and set things down as they
see them. If these powders have any pharmacal virtue
—other than that of Seidlitz—it is likely to be relative,
not absolute. I mean, it is remarkable that they
should have been written at all: remarkable that any
newspaper should take the pains to offer space to
speculations of this sort. I have not scrupled, on oc-
casion, to chaff some of the matters newspapers are
supposed to hold sacred. And it is my privilege, by
the way, to say my gratitude and affection to Mr.
Edwin F. Gay, editor of the New York *Evening Post*,
under whose jurisdiction these were written. With
the generosity of the ideal employer he has encouraged
my ejaculations even when he did not agree with
them.

But a columnist (it is frequently said) is not a real
Newspaper Man: he is only a deboshed Editorial
Writer, a fallen angel abjected from the secure heaven
of anonymity. That is true. The notable increase,
in recent years, of these creatures, has been held to be
a sign that the papers required more scapegoats, or
safety valves through whom readers might blow off

Dedication

their disrespect. And that by posting these innocent effigies as decoys, the wicked press might go about its privy misdeeds with more security, and conspire unobserved with the dangerous minions of Capital (or Labour, or the Agrarian Bloc).

However that may be, and unsuspecting whether intended by his scheming employer as a decoy, or a doormat, or a gargoyle, or a lightning rod (how is he to know, never having been given instruction of any sort except to go ahead and write as he pleases?) the columnist pursues his task and gradually distils a philosophy of his own out of his duties. Oddly enough, instead of growing more cautious by reason of his exposure, he becomes almost dangerously candid. He knows that if he is wrong he will be set right the next morning by a stack of letters varying in number according to the nature of his indiscretion. If he is wrong about *shall* and *will*, he will get five letters of reproof. If about some nautical nicety, ten letters. If about the Republican Party, twenty letters. If about food, thirty-two. If about theology or Ireland, sixty to seventy. In all cases most of these letters will be wittier and wiser than anything he could have composed himself. Surely there is no other walk of life in which mistakes are so promptly retrovolant.

I have christened these soliloquies after dear old Sir Kenelm Digby's famous nostrum, the Powder of Sympathy. But in spite of its amiable name and properties that powder was not a talcum. Its basis was vitriol; and I fear that in some of these prescrip-

[vii]

Dedication

tions I have mixed a few acid crystals. It was either Lord Bacon or Don Marquis (two deep thinkers whose maxims are occasionally confounded in my mind) who told a story about a dog of low degree who made his reputation by biting a circus lion—thinking him only another dog, though a large one. Two or three times herein I have snapped at circus lions; and probably escaped only because the lion was too proud to return the indenture. Let it be remembered, though, that often you may love a man even while you dispute with him.

But the chief consideration (Frank and Felix) that seems to emerge from our friendship is that the eager squabbles of critics and littérateurs are of minor account; that the great thing is to circulate freely in the surrounding ocean of inexhaustible humanity, enjoying with our own eyes and ears the gay and tragic richness of life. We have had expeditions together, not commemorated in print, that have been both doctrine and delight. The incident of the Five-Dollar Bill we hid in a certain bookshop will recur to your minds; the day spent in New York Harbour aboard Tug Number 18, and her skipper's shrewd, endearing sagacity. Then consider the Mystery of the House on 71st Street; the smell of Gorgonzola cheese on a North River pier; the taste of *asti spumante;* the arguments on the Test of Courage! These are matters it pleases me to set down, just as a secret among us. And though I am (you are aware) no partisan of the telephone, there are especially two voices I have learned to hear with a thrill. They say: *"Hello! This is Frank;"* or *"Hello!*

Dedication

This is Felix!" And I reply with honest excitement, for so often those voices are an announcement of Adventure.

Give me a ring soon.

CHRISTOPHER MORLEY.

New York City,
November 24, 1922.

CONTENTS

Contents

THE POWDER OF
SYMPATHY

AN OXFORD SYMBOL

WHEN in October, 1910, we arrived, in a hansom, at the sombre gate of New College, Oxford; trod for the first time through that most impressive of all college doorways, hidden in its walled and winding lane; timidly accosted Old Churchill, the whiskered porter, most dignitarian and genteel of England's Perfect Servants; and had our novice glimpse of that noble Front Quad where the shadow of the battlemented roof lies patterned across the turf—we were as innocently hopeful, modestly anxious for learning and eager to do the right thing in this strange, thrilling environment as ever any young American who went looking for windmills. No human being (shrewd observers have remarked) is more beautifully solemn than the ambitious Young

[1]

The Powder of Sympathy

American. And, indeed, no writer has ever attempted to analyze the shimmering tissue of inchoate excitement and foreboding that fills the spirit of the juvenile Rhodes Scholar as he first enters his Oxford college. He arrives with his mind a gentle confusion of hearsay about Walter Pater, Shelley, boat races, Mr. Gladstone, Tom Brown, the Scholar Gypsy, and Little Mr. Bouncer. Kansas City or Sheboygan indeed seem far away as he crosses those quadrangles looking for his rooms.

But even Oxford, one was perhaps relieved to find, is not all silver-gray mediæval loveliness. The New Buildings, to which Churchill directed us, reached through a tunnel and a bastion in a rampart not much less than a thousand years elderly, were recognizably of the Rutherford B. Hayes type of edification. Except for the look-off upon gray walls, pinnacles, and a green tracery of gardens, and the calculated absence of plumbing (a planned method of preserving monastic hardiness among light-minded youth), the immense cliff of New Buildings might well have been a lobe of the old Johns Hopkins or a New York theological seminary. At the top of four flights we found our pensive citadel. Papered in blue, upholstered in a gruesome red, with yellow woodwork, and a fireplace which (we soon learned) was a potent reeker. It would be cheerful to describe those two rooms in detail, for we lived in them two years. But what first caught our eye was a little green pamphlet lying on the red baize tablecloth. It was lettered

NEW COLLEGE, OXFORD
Information and Regulations
Revised October, 1910

An Oxford Symbol

Our name was written upon it in ink, and we immediately sat down to study it. Here, we thought, is our passkey to this new world of loveliness.

First we found the hours of college chapel. Then, "All Undergraduates are required to perform Exercises." In our simplicity we at first supposed this to be something in the way of compulsory athletics, but then discovered it to mean intellectual exercises. Fair enough, we thought. That is what we came for.

"Undergraduates are required, as a general rule, to be in College or their Lodgings by 11 p. m., and to send their Strangers out before that time. . . . No Undergraduate is allowed to play on any musical instrument in College rooms except between the hours of 1 and 9 p. m., unless special leave has been obtained beforehand from the Dean. . . . No games are allowed in the College Quadrangles, and no games except bowls in the Garden." Excellent, we meditated; this is going to be a serious career, full attention to the delights of the mind and no interruption by corybantic triflers.

"A Term by residence means pernoctation within the University for six weeks in Michaelmas or in Hilary Term, and for three weeks in Easter or in Trinity (or Act) Term." . . . We felt a little uncertain as to just what time of year Hilary and Act happened. But we were not halting, just now, over technicalities. We wanted to imbibe, hastily, the general spirit and flavour of our new home. . . . "Every member of the College is required to deposit Caution-money. Commoners deposit £30, unless they signify in writing their intention to pay their current Battels weekly; in this case they deposit £10. An undergraduate battling terminally cannot withdraw part of his Caution-money and become a weekly battler without the authority of his parent or guardian." We at once decided that it was best to be a weekly battler. Battling, incidentally, is a word that we believe exists only at Eton and Oxford; dictionaries tell us that it comes from "an obsolete verb meaning to fatten." Sometimes, however, in dispute with the Junior Bursar, it comes near its more usual sense. We wondered, in our young American pride, whether we were a Commoner? We were pleased to note, however, that the alternative classification was not a Lord but a Scholar.

We skimmed along through various other instructions. "A fine of 1s. is charged to the owner of any bicycle not put away before midnight." The owner, or the bicycle, we mused? Never mind—we would soon learn. Coals and faggots, we noted, were variable in price. "The charge for a cold bath is 2d., for a hot 4d., inclusive of bath-towel." The duties of a mysterious person named as the Bedmaker (but always, in actual speech, the Scout) were punctually outlined. But now we found ourself coming to Kitchen, Buttery, and Store-Room Tariffs. This, evidently, was the pulse of the machine. With beating heart we read on, entranced:

Beer, Mild............half-pint		$1\frac{1}{2}$
Beer, Mixed............	"	2
Beer, Strong............	"	$2\frac{1}{2}$
Beer, Treble X..........glass		3

An Oxford Symbol

Beer, Lager. . . . . pint   6
Stout. . . . . .half-pint   2
Cider. . . . .   "   1½

There was something significant, we felt by instinct,
in the fact that Treble X was obtainable only by the
glass. Vital stuff, evidently. Our education was
going to come partly in casks, perhaps? In the Kitchen
Tariff we read, gloatingly, magnificent syllables. *Grilled
Sausages and Bacon*, commons, 1/2. *Devilled Kidneys*,
commons, 1/. (A "commons," we judged, was a
large portion; if you wanted a lesser serving, you or-
dered a "small commons.") *Chop with Chips*, 11d.
Grilled Bones, 10d. *Kedgeree*, plain or curried, com-
mons, 9d. (Oh noble kedgeree, so nourishing and in-
expensive, when shall we taste your like again?)
Herrings, Bloaters, Kippers, each 3d. (To think that,
then, we thought the Junior Bursar's tariff was a bit
steep.) Jelly, Compôte of Fruit, Trifle, Pears and
Cream. Creams . . . commons, 6d. "Gentle-
men's own birds cooked and served . . . one
bird, 1/. Two birds, 1/6."

We went on, with enlarging appreciation, to the
Store Room and Cellar Tariffs: Syphons, Seltzer or
Soda-water, 4½d. Ginger-beer, per bottle, 2d. Cakes:
Genoa, Cambridge, Madeira, Milan, Sandringham,
School, each 1/. Foolscap, per quire, 10d. Quill
Pens, per bundle, 1/6. Cheroots, Cigars, Tobacco,
Cigarettes—and then we found what seemed to be the
crown and cream of our education, LIST OF WINES.

Port, 4/ per bottle. Pale Sherry, 3/. Marsala, 2/.

[5]

The Powder of Sympathy

Madeira, 4/. Clarets: Bordeaux 1/6. St. Julien, 2/. Dessert 4/. Hock or Rhenish Wine: Marcobrunner, 4/. Niersteiner, 3/. Moselle, 2/6. Burgundy, 2/ and 4/. Pale Brandy, 5/. Scotch Whisky, 4/. Irish Whisky, 4/. Gin, 3/. Rum, 4/.

It is really too bad to have to compress into a few paragraphs such a wealth of dreams and memories. We sat there, with our little pamphlet before us, and looked out at that great panorama of spires and towers. We have always believed in falling in with our environment. The first thing we did that afternoon was to go out and buy a corkscrew. We have it still—our symbol of an Oxford education.

SCAPEGOATS

THE man who did most (I am secretly convinced)
to deprive American literature of some really
fine stuff was Mr. John Wanamaker. It was in his
store, some years ago, that I bought a kind of cot-bed or
couch, which I put in one corner of my workroom and
on which it is my miserable habit to recline when I
might be getting at those magnificent writings I have
planned. Every evening I pile up the cushions and
nestle there with *The Gentle Grafter* or some detective
story (my favourite relaxation), saying to myself:
"Just ten minutes of loafing". . . .

But perhaps Messrs. Strawbridge and Clothier (also
of Philadelphia) are equally at fault. When I wake up,
on my Wanamaker divan, it is usually about 2 A. M.
Not too late, even then, for a determined spirit to make

The Powder of Sympathy

incision on its tasks. But I find myself moving towards a very fine white-enamelled icebox which I bought from Strawbridge and Clothier in 1918. With that happy faculty of self-persuasion I convince myself it is only to see whether the pan needs emptying or the doors latching. But by the time I have scalped a blackberry pie and eroded a platter of cold macaroni *au gratin*, of course work of any sort is out of the question.

So do the Philistines of this world league themselves cruelly against the artist, plotting temptation for his carnal deboshed instincts, joying to see him succumb. Once the habit of yielding is established, Wanamaker, Strawbridge and Clothier (dark trio of Norns) have it their own way. Just as surely as robins will be found on a new-mown lawn, as certainly as bonfire smoke veers all round the brush pile to find out the eyes of the suburban leaf burner, so inevitably do the Divan and the Icebox exert their cruel dominion over us when we ought to be pursuing our lovely and impossible dreams. Wanamaker and Strawbridge and Clothier have blue-prints of the lines of fissure in our frail velleity. As William Blake might have said:

> Let Flesh once get a lead on Spirit,
> It's hard for Soul to reinherit:
> When supper's laid upon a plate
> Mind might as well abdicate.

But one of the things I think about, just before I drop off to sleep on that couch, is My Anthology. Like

Scapegoats

every one else, I have always had an ambition to compile an anthology of my own; several, in fact. One of them I call in my own mind *The Book of Uncommon Prayer*, and imagine it as a kind of secular breviary, including many of those beautiful passages in literature expressing the spirit of supplication. This book, however, it will take years to collect; it will be entirely non-sectarian and so truly religious that many people will be annoyed. People do not care much for books of real beauty. That anthology edited by Robert Bridges, for instance—*The Spirit of Man*—how many readers have taken the trouble to hunt it out?

But the *Uncommon Prayer Book* is not the kind of anthology I have in mind at the moment. What I need is a book that would boil down the best of all the books I am fond of and condense it into a little bouillon cube of wisdom. I have always had in mind the possibility that I might go travelling, or the house might burn down, or I might have to sell my library, or something of that sort. I should like to have the meat and essence of my favourites in permanent form, so that wherever I were I could write to the publisher and get a fresh copy.

This thought came with renewed emphasis the other day when I was talking to Vachel Lindsay. He was saying that he had lately been rereading Swinburne, for the first time in nearly twenty years, and was grieved to see how the text of the poet had become corrupted in his memory. He had been misquoting Swinburne for years and years, he said, and the errors had been growing more and more firmly into his mind. That led

[9]

The Powder of Sympathy

me to think, suppose we had only memory to rely on,
how long would the text of anything we loved remain
unblurred? Suppose I were on a desert island and
yearned to solace myself by spouting some of the son-
nets of Shakespeare? How much could I recapture?
Honestly, now, and with no resort to the book on the
shelf at my elbow, let me try an old friend:

Let me not to the marriage of true minds
Admit impediments. Love is not love
That alters when it alteration finds
Or bends with the remover to remove.
Oh no, it is an ever-fixed mark
That looks on tempests and is never shaken—
Love is the star to every wandering bark
Whose worth's unknown, although his height be taken.

Then there's something about a sickle, but I can't
for the life of me quite get it. Presently I'll look it up
in the book and see how near I came.

Before opening the Shakespeare, however, let's have
one more try:

When to the sessions of sweet silent thought
I summon up remembrance of things past,
I wail the lack of many a thing I sought
. . . my dear time's waste——

And all the rest of that sonnet that I can think of is
something about "death's dateless night." A pretty
poor showing. Of course, I should do better on a
desert island: there would be the wide expanse of
shining sand to walk upon, and I could throw myself

into it with more passion and fury. The secret of re-
membering poetry is to get a good barytone start and
obliterate the mind of its current freight of trifles. The
metronomic prosody of the surf would help me, no
doubt, and the placid frondage of the breadfruit trees.
But even so, the recension of Shakespeare's sonnets
that I would write down upon slips of bark would be a
very corrupt and stumbling text. Favourite lines
would be scrambled into the wrong sonnets, and the
whole thing would be a pitiful miscarriage of memory.

The only sagacious conduct of life is to prepare for
every possible emergency. I have taken out life in-
surance, and fire insurance, and burglary insurance, and
automobile insurance. I have always insured myself
against losing my job by taking care not to work too
hard at it, so I wouldn't miss it too bitterly if it were
suddenly jerked from under me. But what have I
done in the way of Literary Insurance? Suppose, to-
morrow, Adventure should carry me away from these
bookshelves? How pleasant to have a little microcosm
of them that I could take with me! And yet, unless I
can shake off the servitude of those three Philadelphia
mandarins, Wanamaker and Strawbridge and Clothier,
I shall never have it.

When I think of the plays that I would have written
if it weren't for those three rascals.

TO A NEW YORKER A HUNDRED YEARS
HENCE

I WONDER, old dear, why my mind has lately been going out towards you? I wonder if you will ever read this? They say that wood-pulp paper doesn't last long nowadays. But perhaps some of my grand-children (with any luck, there should be some born, say twenty-five years hence) may, in their years of tottering caducity, come across this scrap of greeting, yellowed with age. With tenderly cynical waggings of their faded polls, perhaps they will think back to the tra-dition of the quaint vanished creatures who lived and strove in this city in the year of disgrace, 1921. Poor old granfer (I can hear them say it, with that pleasing note of pity), I can just remember how he used to prate about the heyday of his youth. He wrote pieces for some paper, didn't he? Comically old-fashioned stuff my governor said; some day I

To a New Yorker

must go to the library and see if they have any record of it.

You seem a long way off, this soft September morning, as I sit here and sneeze (will hay fever still exist in 2021, I wonder?) and listen to the chime of St. Paul's ring eleven. Just south of St. Paul's brown spire the girders of a great building are going up. Will that building be there when you read this? What will be the Olympian skyline of your city? Will poor old Columbia University be so far downtown that you will be raising money to move it out of the congested slums of Morningside? Will you look up, as I do now, to the great pale shaft of Woolworth; to the golden boy with wings above Fulton Street? What ships with new names will come slowly and grandly up your harbour? What new green spaces will your street children enjoy? But something of the city we now love will still abide, I hope, to link our days with yours. There is little true glory in a city that is always changing. New stones, new steeples are comely things; but the human heart clings to places that hold association and reminiscence. That, I suppose, is the obscure cause of this queer feeling that impels me to send you so perishable a message. It is the precious unity of mankind in all ages, the compassion and love felt by the understanding spirit for those, its resting kinsmen, who once were glad and miserable in these same scenes. It keeps one aware of that marvellous dark river of human life that runs, down and down uncountably, to the unexplored seas of Time.

You seem a long way off, I say—and yet it is but an

[13]

The Powder of Sympathy

instant, and you will be here. Do you know that feeling, I wonder (so characteristic of our city) that a man has in an elevator bound (let us say) for the eighteenth floor? He sees 5 and 6 and 7 flit by, and he wonders how he can ever live through the interminable time that must elapse before he will get to his stopping place and be about the task of the moment. It is only a few seconds, but his mind can evolve a whole honey-comb of mysteries in that flash of dragging time. Then the door slides open before him and that instantaneous eternity is gone; he is in a new era. So it is with the race. Even while we try to analyze our present curiosities, they whiff away and disperse. Before we have time to turn three times in our chairs, we shall be the grandparents and you will be smiling at our old-fashioned sentiments.

But we ask you to look kindly on this our city of wonder, the city of amazing beauties which is also (to any man of quick imagination) an actual hell of haste, din, and dishevelment. Perhaps you by this time will have brought back something of that serenity, that reverence for thoughtful things, which our generation lost—and hardly knew it had lost. But even Hell, you must admit, has always had its patriots. There is nothing that hasn't—which is one of the most charming oddities of the race.

And how we loved this strange, mad city of ours, which we knew in our hearts was, to the clear eye of reason and the pure, sane vision of poetry, a bedlam of magical impertinence, a blind byway of monstrous wretchedness. And yet the blacker it seemed to the

To a New Yorker

lamp of the spirit, the more we loved it with the troubled eye of flesh. For humanity, immortal only in misery and mockery, loves the very tangles in which it has enmeshed itself: with good reason, for they are the mark and sign of its being. So you will fail, as we have; and you will laugh, as we have—but not so heartily, we insist; no one has ever laughed the way your tremulous granfers did, old chap! And you will go on about your business, as we did, and be just as certain that you and your concerns are the very climax of human gravity and worth. And will it be any pleasure to you to know that on a soft September morning a hundred years ago your affectionate great-grandsire looked cheerfully out of his lofty kennel window, blew a whiff of smoke, smiled a trifle gravely upon the familiar panorama, knew (with that antique shrewdness of his) a hawk from a handsaw, and then went out to lunch?

A CALL FOR THE AUTHOR

BUT who will write me the book about New York that I desire? The more I think about it, the more astonished I am that no one attempts it. I don't mean a novel. I would not admit any plot or woven tissue of story to come between the reader and my royal heroine, the City herself. Not to be a coward, should I try to write it myself? It is my secret dream; but, better, it should be written by some sturdy rogue of a bachelor, footfree, living in the very heart of the uproar. Some fellow with a taste and nuance for the vulgar and vivid; a consort of both parsons and bootleggers; a *Beggar's Opera* kind of rascal. I can think of three men in this city who have magnificent powers for such a book; but they are getting perhaps a little elderly—yes, they are over forty! Ginger must be

A Call for the Author

very hot in the mouth of my imagined author. He must be young (dashed if I don't think about 32 is the ideal age to write such a book), but not one of the Extremely Brilliant Young Men. They are too clever; and they are not lonely enough. For this is a lonely job. It's got to be done *solus*, slowly, with an eye only upon the subject. It has got to show the very tremble and savour of life itself.

The man who will write this book will not necessarily enjoy it. To get into the secret of Herself he has got to have a peculiar feeling about her. For years he must have wrestled with her almost as a personal antagonist. He must have vowed, since he first saw her imperial skyline serrated on blue, to make her his own; a mistress worthy of him, and yet he himself her master. But he must know, in his inward, that in the end she triumphs, she tramples down mind and heart and nerve. Loveliest enemy in the world, implacable victor over reason and peace and all the quieter sanities of the spirit, her mad, intolerable beauty crazes or silences the sensitive mind that woos her. If you think this is only fine writing and romantic tall-talk, then you know her only with the eye, not with the imagination. With good reason, perhaps, her poets have, for the most part, kept mum. Enough for them to see and cherish in imagination her little sudden glimpses. A girl, slender, gayly unconscious of admiration, poises on one foot at the edge of the subway platform, leaning over to see if the train is coming. That gallant figure is perhaps something of a symbol of the city's own soul.

There must be many who feel about Herself as I do—

[17]

and, more wisely, are tacit. There are many whose minds have trembled on the steep sills of truth, have felt that golden tremble of reality almost within touch, and rather than mar the half-apprehended fable, have turned troubled away. But there is such poetry in her, and such fine, glorious animal gusto—why is there not some determined attempt to set it down, not with "rhetoricating floscules," but as it is? Day after day one comes to the attack; and returning, as the sloping sunlight and fresh country air flood the dusty red plush of the homeward smoking-car, readmits the expected defeat. Here is a target for you, O generation of snipers. Let us have done with pribbles and prabbles. Who is the man who will write me the book I crave— that vulgar, jocund, carnal, beautiful, rueful book!

Pepys' House at Brampton

MR. PEPYS'S CHRISTMASES

CHRISTMAS being the topic, suppose we call upon Mr. Samuel Pepys for testimony. The imperishable Diarist had as keen a faculty of enjoyment as any man who ever lived. He wrote one of the world's greatest love stories—the story of his own zealous, inquisitive, jocund love of life. Surely it is not amiss to inquire what record be left as to the festival of cheer.

On seven of the nine Christmases in the Diary, Mr. Pepys went to church—sometimes more than once, though when he went twice he admits he fell asleep. The music and the ladies' finery were undoubtedly part

The Powder of Sympathy

of the attraction. "Very great store of fine women there is in this church, more than I know anywhere else about us," is his note for Christmas, 1664. But in that generously mixed and volatile heart there was a valve of honest aspiration and piety. One can imagine him sitting in his pew (on Christmas,1661, he nearly left the church in a huff because the verger didn't come forward to open the pew door for him), his alert mind giving close attention to the sermon of his favourite Mr. Mills, busy with sudden resolutions of virtue and industry, yet happily conscious of any beauty within eyeshot.

The giving of presents was not a large part of Christmas in those days. In 1662 Mr. Gauden gave Pepys "a great chine of beef and three dozen of tongues," but this had its drawbacks. Pepys had to give five shillings to the man who brought it and also half a crown to the porters. Drink and food were the important part of the festival. At Christmas, 1660, Mr. and Mrs. Pepys, with Tom Pepys as guest, enjoyed "a good shoulder of mutton and a chicken." This was a brave Christmas for Mrs. Pepys—she had "a new mantle." We must remember that the fair Elizabeth, though already married five years, was then only twenty years old. Not all Mrs. Pepys's Christmases were as merry as that, I fear. On Christmas, 1663, she was troubled by anxious thoughts——

My wife began, I know not whether by design or chance, to enquire what she should do, if I should by any accident die, to which I did give her some slight answer,

Mr. Pepys's Christmases

but shall make good use of it to bring myself to some
settlement for her sake.

Why haven't the ingenious life insurance advertisers
made use of this telling bit of copy?

Christmas, 1668, seems to have been poor Mrs.
Pepys's worst Yule, but perhaps it was only her natural
feminine frivolity that caused the sadness. Samuel
says:

Dinner alone with my wife, who, poor wretch! sat
undressed all day, till 10 at night, altering and lacing of
a noble petticoat.

This noble petticoat was perhaps to be worn at the
play they attended the next day, "Women Pleased."
What a pleasant Christmas card that scene would
make: Mrs. Pepys sitting, négligée, over the niceties
of her needlework, with Samuel beside her "making
the boy read to me the Life of Julius Cæsar." But
we do not "get" (as the current phrase is) Mrs. Pepys
at all if we think of her as merely the irresponsible girl.
For, at Christmas, '66, we read:

Lay pretty long in bed, and then rose, leaving my
wife desirous to sleep, having sat up till 4 this morning
seeing her maids make mince-pies.

Ah, we have no such mince pies nowadays. Mrs.
Pepys's mince pies were evidently worthy the tradition
of that magnificent delicacy, for at Christmas, 1662,

when Elizabeth was ill abed, Samuel records—with an evident touch of regret—that he had to "send abroad" for one.

Which brings us back to the Christmas viands. In 1662, besides the mince pie from abroad, he "dined by my wife's bedside with great content, having a mess of brave plum-porridge and a roasted pullet." We are tempted to think 1666 was Samuel's best Christmas. Parson Mills made a good sermon. "Then home and dined well on some good ribs of beef roasted and mince pies; only my wife, brother, and Barker, and plenty of good wine of my own, and my heart full of true joy." After dinner they had a little music; and he spent the evening making a catalogue of his books ("reducing the names of all| my books to an alphabet"), which is probably the happiest task a man of Pepys's temperament could enjoy.

Christmas Eve, 1667, was evidently a cheerful evening. Mr. Pepys stopped in at the Rose Tavern for some "burnt wine"; walked round the city in the moonlight, and homeward early in the morning in such content that "I dropped money in five or six places, which I was the willinger to do, it being Christmas Day, and so home, and there find my wife in bed, and Jane and the maid making pies." The evening of that Christmas Mrs. Pepys read aloud to him—*The History of the Drummer of Mr. Mompesson*, apparently a kind of contemporary Phillips Oppenheim—"a strange story of spies, and worth reading, indeed." It was only in 1660 that the Christmas cheer was a little too much for our

Mr. Pepys's Christmases

Diarist. December 27, 1660, "about the middle of the night I was very ill—I think with eating and drinking too much—and so I was forced to call the maid, who pleased my wife and I in her running up and down so innocently in her smock."

It is painful to this tracker of Mr. Pepys's vestiges to note that on Christmas Day, 1662, Bishop Morley at the Chapel Royal "made but a poor sermon." The Bishop apparently rebuked the levity of the Court. "It was worth observing how far they are come from taking the reprehensions of a Bishop seriously, that they all laugh in the chapel when he reflected on their ill-actions and courses. He did much press us to joy in these public days of joy, and to hospitality; but one that stood by whispered in my ear that the Bishop do not spend one groat to the poor himself." In 1665 we fear that Samuel indulged himself in church with some rather cynical thoughts:

Saw a wedding in the church, and the young people so merry one with another; and strange to see what delight we married people have to see these poor fools decoyed into our condition, every man and woman gazing and smiling at them.

One could continue for some space recounting the eupeptic Pepys in his Christmas merriments—so large an edifice of pleasing conjecture can be built upon even his slightest notes. One observes, for instance, that on December 27, 1664, when "my wife and all her folks" came "to make Christmas gambols," Samuel left the

[23]

The Powder of Sympathy

party and went to bed. This was very different from his usual habit when there was fun going. He was annoyed also that on this occasion his wife revelled all night, not coming to bed until 8 the next morning, "which vexed me a little, but I believe there was no hurt in it at all, but only mirth."

So we take leave of the Christmases of the Pepyses; 1668 is the last one recorded—the time when Elizabeth stayed at home all day altering her petticoat. After supper, the boy played some music on the lute, and Samuel's mind was "in mighty content." Let us think kindly of the good fellow; and not forget that he coined one of the enduring phrases of English literature —a phrase that is no such ineffective summary of all the lives of men—*And so to bed.*

CHILDREN AS COPY

TITANIA said: "You haven't written a poem about the baby yet."

It is quite true. She is now thirteen months old, and has not yet had a poem written about her. Titania considers this deplorable. The first baby was hardly a week old before all sorts of literary studies were packing the mails, speeding to such editors as were known to be prompt pay. (I hope, indeed I hope, you never saw that astounding essay—published anonymously in *Every Week* which expired soon after —called "The Expectant Father," which was written when the poor urchin was some twenty-four hours old. It was his first attempt to earn money for his parent. If any

The Powder of Sympathy

child ever paid his own hospital bills—C. O. D., as you might say—it was he. I believe in bringing up my children to be self-supporting.)

And the second baby was only three weeks old when the first poem about *her* was written.

But here is this third morsel, thirteen months old and no poem yet. Titania, I say, considers this a kind of insult to the innocent babe. No, not at all, my dear. I admit that it would be very helpful if H. (I will call her that, for *baby* is a word that cannot be repeated in print very often without all hands growing maudlin; and I don't like to use her own name, which seems too personal; just remember, then, that H. stands for a small brown-eyed creature who is still listed in the Bureau of Records of the Department of Health [certificate No. 43515, *anno* 1920] as *Female Morley*, because when the birth was registered by the doctor her name had not been decided, and ever since then I have been too busy to go round to call on Dr. Copeland, the Health Commissioner, and ask him to have her more specifically enrolled)—I admit it would be very helpful if she were to turn to and lend a hand in paying the coal bill by having some verses written about herself. I have looked at her with admiration every day for these thirteen months, trying, as one might say, to get some angle on her that would lead to a poem. She does not seem very angular.

I insist that my not having written a poem about her is really very creditable. Titania seems to think that it implies my having become, in some sense, blasé about children. Again, not so, not so at all. I must

[26]

Children as Copy

confess that in my enthusiasm I rather made use of the two older urchins as copy. But H., droll infant that she is, is too subtle for me. I'll come to that in a minute.

I talked all this matter over (being of a cautious turn, and fond of getting experienced advice) with two eminent author-parents—Mr. Tom Masson and Mr. Tom Daly—long ago, before Titania and I began putting on heirs. Both these gentlemen have made a lot of use of their children in earning, or at any rate gaining, a living. Their advices coincided. I myself was worried, but Mr. Tom Masson insisted that there was nothing like having offspring as a source of copy; he said that he would pay ten cents a word, in *Life*, for anything about the then shortly arriving urchin. (He said it would be fifteen cents a word if it was a girl, because girls cost you so much more later on. He has had experience in that matter, I believe.) Mr. Tom Daly, who has run rather to boys, said very much the same thing; but he was not in a position to buy my stuff, so I paid less attention to him.

But to get back to H. There never was a more enchanting infant. Mr. Walter de la Mare, who is also an authority, has written me delightful letters about her, although he has never seen her. But even a prose letter from a poet like Mr. de la Mare is more valuable, I think, than an actual poem from most other poets, so darling H. cannot say she has been neglected. But she is much too delicious for me to be able to sit down easily and write something that would do her justice. The night before she was born her mother and I did two

The Powder of Sympathy

things. We went to Huyler's for chocolate ice-cream soda, and we read aloud Bernard Shaw's autobiography, which is printed in Frank Harris's *Contemporary Portraits*. I dislike to bring Mr. Harris into this, for certainly I can think of no one who has less in common with H., that celestial nugget. But I have to tell the truth, don't I? Mr. Harris wrote an essay about Shaw; and Shaw, feeling that it was not adequate, wrote a really amusing sketch to show how Harris should have done it. Well, there is something symbolic about this, for H. is as sweet as anything Huyler ever compounded; and she is even more enigmatic than Shaw. (I can see now it should have been Page and Shaw instead of Huyler.)

But I feel that pretty soon I shall be writing a poem about her. I have felt it coming for some time. But it has got to *come;* I am not going to bring it. That shows how I have matured by associating with H. Sometimes I wish I could hire a really great poet to write about her. Swinburne might do for the rough draft. "Oh, what a bee-yootiful babby!" he used to cry when he saw them in their prams up at Putney—so, I think, Max Beerbohm describes. But I should want to have his rough draft polished and refined by someone else. I can only think of Mr. Walter de la Mare. He alone has just the right insight. For babies thirteen months old —the best age of all—must not be treated condescendingly, nor fulsomely, nor adoringly, nor sugarishly. William Blake, if left alone in the room with H., would have understood her. What an infant, I give you my word! Living with children is largely a contest of en-

Children as Copy

durance. It is a question of which one can tire the other out first. (This is a great secret; never before made plain.) Start in early in the morning, and take things with a rush. If you are strong, austere, resolute, you may be able to wear them down and exhaust them by dusk. If you can do so, without prostrating yourself, then you may get them to bed safely and have a few hours of cheerful lassitude. But take every possible advantage. Let them run and frolic, yourself sitting down as much as you can. Favour yourself, and snatch a little rest while they are not looking. Even so, the chances are you will crack first.

This applies to older children; after they gain the use of their limbs and minds. But H. has not reached that harrowing stage. Placable, wise, serene, she sits in her crib. She has four teeth (beauties). To hear her cry is so rare that I hardly know what her voice of sorrow sounds like. Sometimes, for an instant, she looks a little frightened. Then I like her best, for I know she is human, and has in her the general capsule of frailty.

You may be quite sure of one thing, I shall never print that poem unless I feel that it comes somewhere near doing her justice.

HAIL, KINSPRIT!

THE keenest pleasure in life, of course, is to find a Kindred Spirit—one whose mind glows and teeters with delight at the same queer things that rouse us to excitement. We have just found one, and yet we shall never know him, except by his address, which is Y. 1926, the *Times*, E. C. 4, London. For we are much too busy to write to any one, even to a Kindred Spirit.

We will tell you *why* we feel sure he is a Kindred Spirit; but in parenthesis, it was Mr. Pearsall Smith who lamented the fact that the English language contains no satisfactory word for "a person who is enthusiastic about the same things that you are enthusiastic about." It is too grossly clumsy to say *fellow-fan* or *co-enthusiast;* so Mr. Smith, a philologist of charming finesse (have you read his little book *The English Language* published by Henry Holt?) boldly proposed to fill the vacancy by coining the word *milver*. This, he

Hail, Kinsprit!

said, would be useful to poets, since there is no rhyme in English for *silver*.

The word *milver*, alas, leaves us cool, in spite of its usefulness as a rhyme. It does not strike down in the great subsoil of the language—the dark deep skein of inherited word-roots from which our present meanings blossom and put forth. We suggest—without much thought—a mere contraction. How would *kinsprit* do? We rather like the look of it; it has a droll, benign, elvish appearance as we put it down. A couplet occurs to us—

> *They pledged their bond with joyful oath—*
> *A kinsprit passion knit them both.*

That shows you it could be used as an adjective as well. Come, now, if we all pull together very likely we can get Messrs. Merriam to put it in the next edition of Webster:

Kinsprit, *n* and *a*. (orig. obscure: perh. contracted from kin[dred] sprit[e])—A fellow-enthusiast, one impassioned with the same zeal or hobby or enthusiasm.

The reason why we know that Y. 1926 is a kinsprit is in the following notice in the *Personal* column of the London *Times*:

Lost in Taxi last week, SMALL PORTFOLIO containing colour diagrams and newspaper print of Lamb's portrait of Lytton Strachey. Finder rewarded. Y. 1926, The *Times*, E. C. 4.

[31]

The Powder of Sympathy

Well, well, we say to ourself: then there is one other person in the world who felt just as we did about that gloriously entertaining portrait of Mr. Strachey, and who carried it about with him just as we did ours, clipped from the *Manchester Guardian*. But we are luckier than poor Y. 1926, because in an access of enthusiasm we wrote to Mr. Henry Lamb, the artist, and begged from him a photo-print of the picture, which is in front of us now. We think that Mr. Alfred Harcourt, Mr. Strachey's publisher, should implore the loan of the canvas for a few months, and have it exhibited in a Fifth Avenue window where we could all have a good look at it.

We are consumed with curiosity to know more about Y. 1926—where he was going in that taxi, and what the colour diagrams were (they sound interesting) and what are his general comments on life?

ROUND MANHATTAN ISLAND

WE WERE talking with an American who had just come back after living several years in Europe. He expressed with some dismay his resensitized impression of the furious ugliness and clamour of American life; the ghastly wastes of rubbish and kindling-wood suburbs fringing our cities; and suggested that the trouble is that we have little or no instinctive sense of beauty.

To which we replied that perhaps the truth of it is that the American temperament is more likely to see opportunities for beauty in large things than in small. But we were both talking bosh. Only an extraordinarily keen and trained philosophic perception—e. g., a Santayana—can discuss such matters without gibbering. A recent book on young American intellectualism recurs to us as an example of the futility of undigested

The Powder of Sympathy

prattle about æsthetics. Even the word *æsthetics* itself has come to have a windy savour by reason of much sophomore talk.

But, though we have laid by our own copy of that particular book as a permanent curio in the realm of well-meant gravity, its author was obeying a sound and praisable instinct in trying to think about these things— beauty, imagination, the mind's freedom to create, the meaning of our civilization. We are all compelled to such an attempt: shallow, unversed, clumsily intuitive, we grope into them because we are sincerely hungry to understand. The same wise, brave, gracious spirit that moved Mr. Montague to write his exquisite book *Disenchantment* is tremulously and tentatively alert in thousands of less competent minds. And we, for our own part, grow just a little impatient with those who are quick to damn this wildly energetic and thronging civilization because it shows a poverty of settled, tranquil loveliness. We look out of our window into this morning where Mrs. Meynell's "wind of clear weather" tosses the Post Office flags and the rooftop plumes of steam; we see the Woolworth pinnacle hanging over our head—and ask, is it possible that this great spectacle breathes from her towers only the last enchantments of a muddled age?

Aristotle remarked that "the flute is not an instrument which has a good moral effect; it is too exciting." And very likely New York civilization falls under the same reproach. But even if it is all madness, what a gallant raving! You cannot see the beauty in anything until you love it for its own sake. Take the sightseeing

[34]

Round Manhattan Island

boat round Manhattan if you want to get a mental synthesis of this strangest of islands. From a point in the East River off Coenties Slip you will see those cubed terraces of building rising up and upward, shelves and ledges of rectangular perspective like the heaven of a modernist painter. Nor do we deny the madness and horror. Farther up the river you will see the ragged edges of the city, scows loading their tons of jetsam and street scourings, wizened piers, grassless parks, all the pitiful makeshift aquatics of the Harlem region. And yet, all along that gruesome foreshore, boys—and girls, too—bathing gayly in the scum-water, flying ragged kites from pier-bollards, merry and naked on slides of rock or piles of barrels. Only on the three grim islands of Blackwell, Ward, and Randall will you see any touch of beauty. There, grass and trees and beds of canna and salvia (the two great institutional flowers) to soothe the criminal and the mad. When your mind or your morals or your muscles give way, the city will allow you a pleasant haven of greenery and air. It is odd to see the broad grounds of the Children's Hospital—on Randalls Island, is it?—with no child in sight; but across the river the vile and scabby shore is thick with them. And the bases of the Harlem swing-bridges, never trod by any one, are carefully grassed and flowered.

So the history of every modern city consists of a painful, slow retracing of its errors, an attempt to undo painfully and at vast expense the slattern stupidities it has allowed to accumulate. But to see only these paradoxes and uglinesses is to see less than the whole.

The Powder of Sympathy

He cannot have lived very long or thoughtfully with humanity for neighbour who does not ruefully accept greeds and blindnesses as part of its ineradicable habit. It takes a strong stretch of the imagination to grasp this island entire; to see, even in its very squalors and heedlessnesses, an integral portion of its brave teeming life. You must love it for what it is before you have a right to love it for what it may be. We have never been able to think this thing out, but there seems to us to be some vital essence, some miraculous tremor of human energy and folly in the whole scene that condones and justifies the ugliness. It is queer, but the hideous back-lots of the city do not trouble us so greatly: we have a feeling that they are on their way towards being something else. We do not praise them, but we feel in an obscure way they are part of the picture. Zealous passion and movement always present, to the eye of dispassion, aspects either grotesque or terrible, according to that eye's focus. In this ugly hurly-burly we feel daily (though we cannot define it) that there is a beauty so overriding that it does not depend on beautiful particulars. And, to feel that beauty fully, one must discard all hankerings to improve humanity, or to preach to it, or even understand it—simply (as Uncle Remus said) "make a great 'miration"—accept it as it thrillingly is, and admire.

THE UNKNOWN CITIZEN

WE SHALL never forget being in Washington when the great celebration was held in honour of the Unknown Citizen.

The day was proclaimed a National Fête. On that day the Unknown Citizen—chosen after long investigation by a secret committee sworn to silence—arrived at the Union Station. He and his wife had been quietly lured away from their home on a plausible pretext and then kidnapped into a gaudy special train, where everything had been explained to them. Halts had been made at big cities en route for the crowds to pay homage.

It would take too long to describe the clever selective

The Powder of Sympathy

process by which the Citizen had been chosen. Suffice it to say that he was a typical *homo Americanus*—a worthy and slightly battered creature, who had raised a family of four children and plugged along at his job and paid his taxes and cranked his flivver and set up a radio on the roof and planted sunflowers in the back yard and lent his wife a hand at the washing and frequently mended the kitchen stove-pipe. He had never broken open the china pigs containing the children's money.

We saw him arrive at the great station in Washington. He was strangely troubled and anxious, a bit incredulous, too, believing this was all some sort of put-up job. Also, somewhere on the train he had lost one of his elastic sleeve-suspenders, and one cuff kept on falling round his wrist. He walked uneasily along the red velvet carpet and was greeted by President Harding and the Ambassadors of Foreign Powers. Mr. Sousa's band was there, and struck up an uproarious anthem composed for the occasion. The tactful committee of Daughters of the American Bourgeoisie had made all arrangements and taken all possible precautions. It had been feared that perhaps the Citizen's Wife might be overcome, and an ambulance was waiting behind potted palms in case of any emergency. But it is always the unexpected that happens. It was Senator Lodge, who had been appointed to read the telegrams from prominent people, who swooned. President Harding, with kindly readiness, stepped into the breach. As they were handed to him he read aloud the messages from M. Clemenceau, Mr. Lloyd George, William Allen

The Unknown Citizen

White, Samuel Gompers, Dr. Frank Crane, President Ebert, Paul Poiret, M. Paderewski, M. Venizelos, the Archbishop of Canterbury, and Isaac Marcosson. Mr. Harding then spoke in the most friendly and charming way, appraising the value of preserved nationality, the solid virtue of the Founding Fathers, and the services of the Unknown Citizen to his country.

For a moment there was an awkward pause, but the Citizen's Wife, evidently a strong-minded woman, nudged him sharply, and the Citizen tottered forward. Fortunately some New York newspaper men had been on the train with him, and had written a little speech for him to deliver. He read it, a bit tremulously. It stated that he was aware this tribute was not meant for him personally, but for the great body of middle-class citizenship he had been chosen to represent. There was great speculation in the audience as to what part of the country the Citizen came from: his accent was perhaps a trifle Hoosierish, but wiseacres insisted that his general fixings were plainly Sears-Roebuck and not identifiable with any section.

Accompanied by a troop of cavalry and the national colours, the Unknown Citizen was taken to the Capitol, where Congress, convened in joint session, awaited to do him honour. He was presented to the great body by Senator Lodge, who had now completely recovered. After being introduced, the Citizen stammered a few words of embarrassment. During the buffet lunch in the lobbies, however, he began to pluck up heart, for he found the Congressmen very human. He even ventured to express, very politely, a few sentiments about

[39]

The Powder of Sympathy

the bonus, the tariff, the income tax, the shipping subsidy, and the coal strike. Gathering confidence, he might have grown almost eloquent over these topics, but the Senatorial committee, foreseeing trouble, hastened him along to see the gifts that had been sent from all over the world. They were all laid out for inspection. Henry Ford had sent a new sedan, with a self-starter and the arms of the United States gilded on the door. William Randolph Hearst had sent a bound volume of Arthur Brisbane's editorials. The Prince of Wales, perhaps misunderstanding the exact nature of the ceremony, had sent a solid gold punch bowl engraved *Dieu et Mon Drought*. The Premier of New Zealand had sent a live kangaroo. The Bailiff of Angora had sent a large silky goat. Mayor Hylan had sent a signed photograph of himself wearing overalls. The Shipping Board had sent a silver flask. But we have not space for the full list of presents.

Tea was served at the White House. All the *corps diplomatique* were there, and were presented to the Citizen and his Wife. It was a great afternoon. The Marine Band played in the garden; Senator Borah and William Jennings Bryan, beginning to see a sort of prickly heat burn out upon the Unknown Citizen's forehead, tactfully played a tennis match to keep the crowd in good humour. Laddie Boy, wagging his tail vigorously, kept at the Unknown Citizen's heels and did much to cheer him. The Unknown Citizen liked Mr. Harding greatly and found him easy to talk to; but some of the Special Representatives from abroad, such as Mr. Balfour and M. Tardieu, he found difficult.

The Unknown Citizen

The monument in Potomac Park was dedicated at sunset. After that the committee on Savoir Faire, observing the wilted collar of the Unknown Citizen, thought it the truest courtesy to let him escape. We ourself managed to follow him through the crowds. He and his wife looked nervously over their shoulders now and then, but they had shaken off pursuit. At a little stationery store they bought some postcards. Then they went to the movies.

SIR KENELM DIGBY

Sir Kenelm Digby, of whose acquaintance all his contemporaries seem to have been ambitious.

—Dr. Johnson, *Life of Cowley.*

PROHIBITION, I dare say, is going to make fashionable the private compilation of just such delightful works as *The Closet of the Eminently Learned Sir Kenelme Digbie Opened; London, at the Star in Little Britain, 1669.* Sir Kenelm, "the friend of kings and the special friend of queens," crony of such diverse spirits as Bacon, Ben Jonson, and Oliver Cromwell, kept this notebook of his jocund experiments in home brewing and cookery. Just as nowadays a man will

[42]

Sir Kenelm Digby

jot down the formula of some friend's shining success in
the matter of domestic chianti, so did the admirable
Kenelm record "Sir Thomas Gower's Metheglin for
Health," or "My Lord Hollis' Hydromel," or "Sir
John Colladon's Oat-Meal Pap," or "My Lady Diana
Porter's Scotch Collops;" and adding, of course, his
own particular triumphs—e. g., "Hydromel as I Made
it Weak for the Queen Mother," "A Good Quaking
Bag-Pudding," and "To Fatten Young Chickens in a
Wonderful Degree." Sir Kenelm's official duty at the
court of Charles the First was Gentleman of the Bed-
chamber; but if I had been Charles, I should have trans-
ferred him to the Pantry.

The *Closet Opened* (which was not published until
after Sir Kenelm's death; he was born 1603, died 1665)
is the kind of book delightfully apt for the sad, sa-
gacious, and solitary, for one cannot spend an hour in it
without deriving a lively sense of the opulence and
soundness of life. The affectionate attention Sir
Kenelm pays the raisin makes him seem almost a Vol-
steadian figure: in his pages that excellent and power-
ful fruity capsule plays, perhaps for the first time in
history, a heroic and leading rôle. Consider this:

TO MAKE ALE DRINK QUICK

WHEN small Ale hath wrought sufficiently, draw into
bottles; but first put into every bottle twelve good
raisins of the Sun split and stoned. Then stop up the
bottle close and set it in sand (gravel) or a cold dry
Cellar. After a while this will drink exceedingly quick
and pleasant. Likewise take six Wheat-corns, and

[43]

The Powder of Sympathy

bruise them, and put into a bottle of Ale; it will make it exceeding quick and stronger.

Kenelm was not only a good eater; he was a devilish good writer. The fine lusty root of English prose was in him. If this is not true literature, we know it not:

ANOTHER CLOUTED CREAM

Milk your Cows in the evening about the ordinary hour, and fill with it a little Kettle about three quarters full, so that there may be happily two or three Gallons of Milk. Let this stand thus five or six hours. About twelve a Clock at night kindle a good fire of Charcoal, and set a large Trivet over it. When the fire is very clear and quick, and free from all smoak, set your Kettle of Milk over it upon the Trivet, and have in a pot by a quart of good Cream ready to put in at the due time; which must be, when you see the Milk begin to boil simpringly. Then pour in the Cream in a little stream and low, upon a place, where you see the milk simper. . . .

To simper—a word of sheer genius! There are many such in his recipes.

We find the raisin again at work in his directions:

TO MAKE EXCELLENT MEATHE

To every quart of Honey, take four quarts of water. Put your water in a clean Kettle over the fire, and with a stick take the just measure, how high the water cometh, making a notch, where the superficies toucheth the stick. As soon as the water is warm, put in your Honey, and let it boil, skiming it always, till it be very clean; Then put to every Gallon of water, one pound of the best Blew-raisins of the Sun, first clean picked from the stalks, and clean washed. Let them remain

Sir Kenelm Digby

in the boiling Liquor, till they be throughly swollen and
soft; Then take them out, and put them into a Hair-bag,
and strain all the juice and pulp and substance from
them in an Apothecaries Press; which put back into
your liquor, and let it boil, till it be consumed just to
the notch you took at first, for the measure of your water
alone. Then let your Liquor run through a Hair-
strainer into an empty Woodden-fat, which must stand
endwise, with the head of the upper-end out; and there
let it remain till the next day, that the liquor be quite
cold. Then Tun it up into a good Barrel, not filled
quite full, and let the bung remain open for six weeks.
Then stop it up close, and drink not of it till after nine
months.

This Meathe is singularly good for a Consumption,
Stone, Gravel, Weak-sight, and many more things. A
Chief Burgomaster of Antwerpe, used for many years
to drink no other drink but this; at Meals and all times,
even for pledging of healths. And though He were an
old man he was of an extraordinary vigor every way,
and had every year a Child, had always a great appetite
and good digestion; and yet was not fat.

One of good Sir Kenelm's most famous instructions,
which has become fairly well-known, does honour not
only to his delicate taste but also to his religious de-
votion. It is his advice on the brewing of tea—"The
water is to remain upon it no longer than whiles you
can say the *Miserere* Psalm very leisurely." This advice
occurs in the recipe

TEA WITH EGGS

The Jesuite that came from China, Ann. 1664, told
Mr. Waller, That there they use sometimes in this man-
ner. To near a pint of the infusion, take two yolks of

[45]

The Powder of Sympathy

new laid-eggs, and beat them very well with as much fine Sugar as is sufficient for this quantity of Liquor; when they are very well incorporated, pour your Tea upon the Eggs and Sugar, and stir them well together. So drink it hot. This is when you come home from attending business abroad, and are very hungry, and yet have not conveniency to eat presently a competent meal. This presently discusseth and satisfieth all rawness and indigence of the stomack, flyeth suddainly over the whole body and into the veins, and strengthenth exceedingly and preserves one a good while from necessity of eating. Mr. Waller findeth all those effects of it thus with Eggs. In these parts, He saith, we let the hot water remain too long soaking upon the Tea, which makes it extract into itself the earthy parts of the herb. The water is to remain upon it no longer than whiles you can say the *Miserere* Psalm very leisurely. Thus you have only the spiritual parts of the Tea, which is much more active, penetrative, and friendly to nature.

Sometimes, it is true, one suspects Sir Kenelm of a tendency to gild the lily. In the matter of perfuming his tobacco, this was his procedure:—

Take Balm of Peru half an ounce, seven or eight Drops of Oyl of Cinamon, Oyl of Cloves five drops, Oyl of Nutmegs, of Thyme, of Lavender, of Fennel, of Aniseeds (all drawn by distillation) of each a like quantity, or more or less as you like the Odour, and would have it strongest; incorporate with these half a dram of Ambergrease; make all these into a Paste; which keep in a Box; when you have fill'd your Pipe of Tobacco, put upon it about the bigness of a Pin's Head of this Composition.

It will make the Smoak most pleasantly odoriferous,

Sir Kenelm Digby

both to the Takers, and to them that come into the Room; and ones Breath will be sweet all the day after. It also comforts the Head and Brains.

It is a great temptation to go on quoting these seductive formulæ. I feel sure that my tenderer readers would relish instructions for the Beautifying Water or Precious Cosmetick,—for the secret of which ladies of high degree pursued Sir Kenelm all over Europe. (He does not include in the *Closet* any details of the Viper Wine for the Complection which was said to have caused the death of Lady Digby—a rather painful scandal at the time.) But I fear to trespass on your patience. Let me only add that the ambition of the Three Hours for Lunch Club has long been to hold a DIGBY DINNER, at which all the dishes will be prepared as nearly as possible according to Sir Kenelm's prescriptions. The project offers various perplexities, and might even have to be consummated at sea, beyond the hundred-fathom curve. But if it ever comes to pass, the following menu, carefully chosen from Sir Kenelm's delicacies, seems to me promising:—

Portugal Broth, As It Was Made for the Queen
Sack with Clove Gillyflowers
Sucket of Mallow Stalks
A Herring Pye
A Smoothening Quiddany of Quinces
My Lady Diana Porter's Scotch Collops
Mead, from the Muscovian Ambassador's Steward
The Queen Mother's Hotchpot of Mutton
Pease of the Seedy Buds of Tulips
Boiled Rice in a Pipkin

[47]

The Powder of Sympathy

Marmulate of Pippins
Dr. Bacon's Julep of Conserve of Red Roses
Excellent Spinage Pasties
Pleasant Cordial Tablets, Which Strengthen Nature
Small Ale for the Stone
A Nourishing Hachy
Plague Water
Marrow Sops with Wine
My Lord of Denbigh's Almond Marchpane
Sallet of Cold Capon Rosted
My Lady of Portland's Minced Pyes
The Liquor of Life
A Quaking Bag-Pudding
Metheglin for the Colic

But I must not mislead you into thinking that Sir Kenelm was merely a convivial trencherman. His biography as related in the *Encyclopædia Britannica* is as diverting as a novel—more so than many. Infant prodigy, irresistible wooer, privateer, scientist, religious controversialist, astrologer, and a glorious talker, he made a profound impression on the life of his time. But, as so often happens, his name has been carried down to posterity not by the strange laborious treatise he regarded as his opus maximum, but by his chance association with one of the great books of all time. When Digby was under honorable confinement (as a "Popish recusant") at Winchester House, Southwark, in 1642, he was busy there with chemical experiment and the MS. of his *Of Bodies and Mans Soul* (of which more in a moment). Apparently they treated political prisoners with more indulgence in those days. One evening he received a letter from his friend the Earl

[48]

Sir Kenelm Digby

of Dorset, urging him to read a book that was making a stir among the intellectuals. One may think it was perhaps a trifle niggardly of Dorset merely to have recommended the book. To a friend in jail, surely he might (and it was just before Christmas) have sent a copy as a present. But the liberality of the Earl is not to be called in question: he had made Sir Kenelm at least one startlingly gracious gift—viz. Lady Digby herself, previously Dorset's mistress. This oddly amusing story, or gossip, may be pursued in Aubrey's *Brief Lives*, a fascinating book (published by the Oxford Press)—a sort of Social Register of seventeenth century England.

"Late as it was" when Sir Kenelm received the letter from his benefactor and colleague, he sent out at once (mark the high spirit of the true inquirer; also the sagacity of seventeenth century booksellers, who kept open at night)—

> To let you see how the little needle of my Soul is throughly touched at the great Loadstone of yours, and followeth suddenly and strongly, which way soever you becken it . . . . I sent presently (as late as it was) to *Pauls* Church-yard, for this Favourite of yours, *Religio Medici:* which found me in a condition fit to receive a Blessing; for I was newly gotten into my Bed. This good natur'd creature I could easily perswade to be my Bed-fellow, and to wake with me, as long as I had any edge to entertain my self with the delights I sucked from so noble a conversation.

Rarely have the pleasures of reading in bed had such durable result. The following day he spent in pouring

The Powder of Sympathy

out a long, spirited and powerful letter to Dorset (75 printed pages) which has become famous as *Observations upon Religio Medici*, and a few years later was included as a supplement to that book—where it still remains in most editions. In this tumbling out of his honourable meditations and excitements, Sir Kenelm took issue pretty smartly with Dr. Browne on a number of points, particularly in regard to his own special hobby of Immortality. He, just as much as the Norwich physician, loved to lose himself in an Altitudo; but in some cloudlands of airy doctrine Browne seemed to him too precise. "The dint of Wit," Digby remarked felicitously of some theological impasse, "is not forcible enough to dissect such tough matter."

These *Observations* are of more than casual importance. Dorset, apparently, took steps (unknown to Digby) to have them published; and report of this coming blast roused Browne to protest courteously against "animadversions" based upon the unauthorized and imperfect version of his book—his own "true and intended Originall" being by this time in the printer's hands. Digby had written his observations without knowing who the author of *Religio* was. The letters that now passed between him and Browne are an exhilarating model of controversy goldenly conducted between gentlemen of the grand manner. "You shall sufficiently honour me in the vouchsafe of your refute," writes Browne, "and I obliege the whole world in the occasion of your Pen." To which Digby, avowing that his comments were written without thought of print and merely as a "private exercitation," charmingly

Sir Kenelm Digby

disclaims any ambition to enter public argument with
so superior a scholar. "To encounter such a sinewy
opposite, or make Animadversions upon so smart a
piece as yours is, requireth such a solid stock and exercise
in school learning. My superficial besprinkling will
serve only for a private letter, or a familiar discourse
with Lady auditors. With longing I expect the com-
ming abroad of the true copy of the Book, whose false
and stoln one hath already given me so much delight."
The delightful remark about lady auditors causes one
to suspect that even in that day the germ of the lecture
passion was moving in circles of high-spirited females.

Digby and Browne were evidently kinsprits. They
were nearly of an age; Browne was a physician, and
Digby—though many considered him a mountebank
and charlatan—had a genuine scientific zeal for med-
ical dabblings. His Powder of Sympathy, a nos-
trum for healing wounds at a distance, has been a
cause of merriment among later generations; but Sir
Kenelm was no fool and I am not at all sure that there
wasn't much excellent sense in his procedure. The
injury itself was washed and kept under a clean band-
age. The Powder of Sympathy was to be prepared
from a paste of vitriol, and the instructions included
necessity for mixing and exposing it in sunshine. Sir
Kenelm was quite aware of the public appetite for
hocus-pocus, and surely there was a touch of anticipa-
tory Christian Science and Coué in his idea of keeping
the patient's mind off the trouble and giving him this
harmless amusement in the open air. For the sympa-
thetic powder, please note, was never to be applied to

The Powder of Sympathy

the wound itself, but only to something carrying the
blood of the injured person—a stained bandage, a
garment, or even the weapon with which the damage
was done. The injury was left to the curative progress
of Nature. This theory of treating not the wound but
the weapon might well be meditated by literary critics.
For instance, when some toxicated energumen publishes
an atrocious book, the best course to pursue is not to
attack the author but to praise Walter de la Mare or
Stella Benson. This may be termed the allopathic
principle in criticism; but few of us are steadfast enough
to adhere to it.

Digby's *Memoirs*—not published until 1827—exhibit
him as the swashbuckler, and amorist by no means
faint. They are amusing enough but give only a carnal
silhouette. Perhaps he did not write the book himself:
there is a vein of burlesque in the narrative that makes
me suspicious. It purports to be an account of Sir
Kenelm's fidelity to his wife, the lovely Venetia; and we
are told that the account was written under Antonian
pressure. Importuned by ladies of much personal
generosity and recklessness, Sir Kenelm austerely re-
tires to a cave and pens this confession of uxorious
loyalty. When you consider that the relations of Sir
Kenelm and Lady Venetia were one of the fashionable
uproars of the day, you begin to guess that the Memoir
(in which all the characters are concealed by romantic
pseudonyms) was an elaborate skit intended for private
circulation, probably the work of some satirical friend.
Exactly so, when any great scandal nowadays is riding
on the front pages of the newspapers, do City Room re-

Sir Kenelm Digby

porters compose humorous burlesques of the printed "stories," and these have delightful currency round the office.

So you will still find legends in print suggesting that Sir Kenelm was a blend of Casanova and Dr. Munyon. He has been attributed what historians used to call "Froude's disease"—an insufficient curiosity as to the total of 2 and 2 when added together. But a man whose memory still makes a page and a half of the *Encyclopædia Britannica* such lively reading, must have had more than mere animal spirits in his make-up. It is easy to find testimony to his potent social and military accomplishments. But the man himself, his earnest scientific passions, his valiant speculation on human destinies, does not emerge from the entries in encyclopædias. For that you must look into his great book *Two Treatises: The Nature of Bodies, and The Nature of Mans Soul* (1658). By the kindness of Mr. Wilbur Macey Stone, generous and astonishingly Elizabethan explorer of old books, I have an original, tawny and most aromatic copy of this queer treasure. The title page of the Second Treatise is endorsed, with a charming use of the aspirates—

SAMUEL MELLOR'S BOOK, December 22th 1792.

> *Samuel Mellor his my Name*
> *and Cheshire is my Nation*
> *and Burton is my Dwellings*
> *Place and Christ is my*
> *Salvation*
> *this Book geven*
> *has A Gift to Samuel Mellor*

The Powder of Sympathy

Sir Kenelm dedicates the volume to his son, in a touching and honourable letter dated "Paris the last of August 1644." "The calamity of this time" (he says) "hath bereft me of the ordinary means of expressing my affection to you; I have been casting about, to find some other way of doing that in such sort, as you may receive most profit by it. Therein I soon pitched upon these Considerations; that Parents owe unto their children, not only material subsistence for their Body, but much more, spiritual contributions to their better part, their Mind." Accordingly, with perfect gravity and that sombre and Latinized eloquence which was the peculiar gift of his century, he proceeds to expound in nearly 600 dense pages his observations on what we would call nowadays physics and psychology. It would be agreeable enough, if I did not fear to weary you, to copy down some of Sir Kenelm's delightful shrewd comments. A few of his section headings will serve to give an idea of his matter. For instance:—

The experience of burning glasses, and of soultry gloomy weather, prove light to be fire.
Philosophers ought not to judge of things by the rules of vulgar people.
The reason why the motion of light is not discerned coming towards us, and that there is some real tardity in it.
The true sense of the Maxim, that Nature abhorreth from vacuity.
The loadstone sendeth forth its emanations spherically. Which are of two kinds: and each kind is strongest in that hemisphere, through whose polary parts they issue out.
The reason why sometimes the same object appears

Sir Kenelm Digby

*through the prism in two places: and in one place more
lively, in the other place more dim.*

*How the vital spirits sent from the brain, do run to the
intended part of the body without mistake.*

*Of the rainbow, and how by the colour of any body, we
may know the composition of the body it self.*

*How things renewed in the fantasie, return with the
same circumstances that they had at first.*

*Why divers men hate some certain meats, and particu-
larly cheese.*

Here, you will agree, was a man who even when he
seems naïf, examined phenomena with his own eyes and
with notable sharpness. Delving into the "crooked
narrow cranies & restrayned flexuous rivolets of
corporeal things" was, he insisted, a "difficult & spiny
affaire;" he was eager to avoid "meer Chymeras and
wild paradoxes," hoped that "by strong abstraction,
and by deep retirement into the closet of judgment"
he might win "a favourable doom" from his readers.
There is no naïveté so dangerous as that of under-
estimating the power of another man's mind. Behind
some of his fanciful suggestions there is an astonishing
agility of conjecture. On the subject of physiology he
is delicious. Hear him (pared down to stark brevity)
on the brain:—

We may take notice that it containeth, towards the
middle of its substance, four concavities, as some do
count them: but in truth, these four, are but one great
concavity, in which four, as it were, divers roomes, may
be distinguished. . . . Now, two rooms of this
great concavity, are divided by a little body, somewhat
like a skin, (though more fryable) which of itself is

The Powder of Sympathy

clear; but there it is somewhat dimmed, by reason that hanging a little slack, it somewhat shriveleth together: and this, Anatomists do call *Septum lucidum*, or speculum. . . .

This part seemeth to me, to be that and onely that, in which the fansie or common sense resideth . . . it is seated in the very hollow of the brain; which of necessity must be the place and receptacle where the species and similitudes of things doe reside, and where they are moved and tumbled up and down, when we think of many things. And lastly, the situation we put our head in, when we think earnestly of any thing, favoureth this opinion: for then we hang our head forwards, as it were forcing the specieses to settle towards our forehead, that from thence they may rebound, and work upon this diaphanous substance.

But it is in the Second Treatise ("Declaring the Nature and Operations of Mans Soul; out of which, The Immortality of Reasonable Souls, is Convinced") that the darling man rises to really dazzling heights. In this mystical, ecstatic and penitential essay he (in Burton's phrase) rectifies his perturbations. He is no longer channeled in the "crooked narrow cranies of corporeal things;" he works from withinward and spirals in happy ether:—

To thee then my soul, I now address my speech. For since by long debate, and toilsom rowing against the impetuous tides of ignorance, and false apprehensions, which overthrow thy banks, and hurry thee headlong down the stream, whiles thou art imprisoned in thy clayie mansion; we have with much ado arrived to aim at some little attome of thy vast greatness; and with the hard and tough blows of strict and wary reasoning, we

[56]

Sir Kenelm Digby

have strucken out some few sparks of that glorious light,
which invironeth and swelleth thee: it is high time, I
should retire my self out of the turbulent and slippery
field of eager strife and litigious disputation, to make my
accounts with thee; where no outward noise may dis-
tract us, nor any way intermeddle between us, excepting
onely that eternal verity, which by thee shineth upon my
faint and gloomy eyes. . . . Existence is that
which comprehendeth all things: and if God be not
comprehended in it, thereby it is, that he is incompre-
hensible of us: and he is not comprehended in it, because
himself is it. . . . Which way soever I look, I lose
my sight, in seeing an infinity round about me: Length
without points: Breadth without Lines: Depth with-
out any surface. All content, all pleasure, all restless
rest, all an unquietness and transport of delight, all an
extasie of fruition.

So don't let any one tell you that Sir Kenelm was only
a seventeenth century epicure and bootlegger.

FIRST IMPRESSIONS OF AN AMIABLE VISITOR

WE THOUGHT of telling you about the things that most interested a British friend of ours during the first hours of his first visit to this country.

Perhaps first of all we should give you an inkling of what kind of chap he is. He's a Welshman, an Oxford man, served in the war as a captain in the Highland Light Infantry, was awarded the Military Cross, is now in the wholesale tobacco business, is an ardent reader, and we daren't mention his name. He's over here to study conditions in the world of tobacco.

We went down the bay and boarded the *Baltic* in the Narrows. We stood with our friend on what a landsman might call the roof while the ship came up the harbour. We pointed out Liberty, as she emerged from the sunlit wintry haze. At first glimpse, coming in from sea, she has rather a forbidding mien—her gesture seems one of warning. Then, as you come nearer, she seems to be holding up a cocktail shaker. But we promised to give our friend's impressions, not our own.

The first things he wanted to have pointed out to

him were the Woolworth Tower and the Brooklyn Bridge. Brooklyn engaged his fancy more than the Jersey shore—probably on account of the Walt Whitman tradition. "I have rather a feeling for Whitman," he said. He was quiet as we passed the long profile of downtown skyscrapers, but we saw that he was inwardly meditating. He wanted to know about all the water tanks on top of the buildings, especially on the Jersey side. "You people seem very keen about water," he said. He was hugely pleased with the way the tugs got the *Baltic* into her berth.

He wondered whether, before landing, we had better dispose of a little toddy he had in his pocket flask. He had heard that if any usquebaugh were found, the officials would confiscate the flask. We agreed that it would be better not to take any chances on this matter. He was greatly surprised and delighted with the rapidity and courtesy of the customs examination. We got away from the pier with no more trouble, he said, than we would have had in arriving at a railway terminal in London.

We took a taxi, bound for Penn. Station, and then decided to prolong the ride by going down Fifth Avenue to Washington Square, and up again. He remarked that the street paving near the docks was no better than it is in Liverpool. He was charmed by the chauffeur's air of camaraderie. The latter, hearing through the open window that this was an exploring expedition, began offering most friendly suggestions as to nice long rides we might take, to Central Park, for instance. "Take him to see the skaters, he'll enjoy that," said

The Powder of Sympathy

the chauffeur. This friendly informality on the part of brakemen, soda jerkers, cab drivers, ticket choppers, shop girls, and all such public servants delighted him.

Madison Square appealed to him, for he is an admirer of O. Henry. "That's where the old tramps sit on the benches, isn't it?" he said. He was anxious to see a "surface car," for he had read about them in *The Four Million*. The L did not seem to interest him so much. In a drug store, he was excited by the little whirling instrument that mixed our "frosted chocolate." The lighting, spaciousness, and attractive display in the department stores tickled him. The Penn. Station gave him extraordinary pleasure. Chiefly, we thought, he was struck by a general spaciousness and lack of hurry everywhere, in the traffic, in the shops, etc. When we asked him what he wanted to see, he said, "I want to see some of you *hustling*." We looked everywhere, but could find no one hustling. Like a candid observer, however, he noticed one thing which is not beneath the attention of any student of human manners. "Your people have rather a fine line in legs," he said.

We pointed proudly to the Public Library (but could not bear to tell him that the City has again cut its appropriation for buying new books). He praised the large windows at the backs of the taxicabs, making it possible to see what was going on behind the car. In Madison Square he was particularly delighted by Diana, who seemed just then to be aiming her gilded arrow at the pale, low-swimming daylight moon. He asked us whether we thought he should subscribe to the *Saturday Evening Post* and the *Literary Digest*. Both these

First Impressions of a Visitor

journals, in some way or other, had come prominently to his attention at his home in Cheshire. *Harper's* and *The Century*, he said, he frequently reads.

He thought it was a bit unfair of the advertisers (this was in the Long Island train) to take advantage of public attention by issuing a card with the announcement NOTICE TO PASSENGERS, looking very like official information, which turned out to be a chewing gum ad. We told him about the card in the subway which says PASSENGERS CHANGE HERE and then adds "to —— Union Suits." This amused him, but we could see that he didn't think it quite sporting. He was highly diverted by the little signs at the subway ticket booths—*Sing Out How Many* and *The Voice with the Smile Wins*. He was quite startled to learn that the author of *Trivia* (one of his favourite books) is an American. He was pleased by the informality of the Long Island conductor, who, seeing a lady friend among the passengers, sat down with her between stations and had a social chat.

Standing at the front of a subway train as it roared through the tunnel from Brooklyn seemed to give him innocent happiness. Again he commented, in the downtown region, on the general air of order and good management in the conduct of the traffic. He could see none of the brutal scurry that he had been taught to expect. Going up the Woolworth Tower was the greatest adventure of these few hours. This, we think, he will not soon forget. He was greatly pleased, being himself a householder, with the American kitchen. He thought it very well planned. Jericho cider he praised

The Powder of Sympathy

without reserve. A revolving apparatus for airing clothes in the back garden pleased him mightily. Delightful fellow, blessings upon him!

It is visits such as his that add to the stock of true international understanding.

IN HONOREM: MARTHA WASHINGTON

AN AMERICAN figure of national consequence has passed away from the scene of her many glories. We refer to Martha Washington, the Independence Hall cat.

When we worked in the old Philadelphia *Ledger* office, and paragraphs were scarce, we had an unfailing recourse. We would go over to the State House (as they call it in its home town), descend to the cool delightful old cellar underneath the hall, and call on Fred Eckersberg, the engineer. We would see Martha sleeking herself on the flagstones by the cellar steps (she was the blackest cat we ever knew, giving off an almost purple lustre in hot sunlight) or perhaps we would have to search her out among the coal bins where she was fixing a layette for the next batch of kittens.   In any case, Martha having been duly admired, Fred Eckersberg would gladly talk about her and tell us what were the latest adventures of her historic life.   Which was always good copy, for Fred, having been on friendly terms with Philadelphia reporters for many years, knew the kind of anecdotes that would please them.   One of Fred's unconscious triumphs was the time he told us of his perplexity about ringing in the New Year in the Independence Hall belfry.   It was about Christmas time, 1919.   "Last January," he said, "I rang One-Nine-One-Nine to welcome in the New Year.   But what am I going to do this time?   How can I ring One-Nine-Two-Nought?"   We told him we saw no way out of it but to start early in the afternoon of New Year's Eve and ring the whole One Thousand Nine Hundred and Twenty tolls.

We could say a good deal about Martha Washington: her kittens are surely the most noble in the land, charter members of the Colonial Felines of America, all born in the Hall, directly underneath the lobby where the Bell stands.   When the most famous brood of all were swaddled, four fine jetty daughters born in November, 1918, Fred christened them Victory, Freedom, Liberty, and Independence.   He paid us the greatest compliment of our life by offering us Victory, but at that time we were living in a small apartment in the city and we didn't think it would be a sufficiently dignified home for such a kitten, who deserved nothing less than a resi-

In Honorem: Martha Washington

dence on the Main Line (Oh, Philadelphia!), with scrapple made on the premises.

But it is time to get down to the point of our story. Martha has left the Hall. Poor Fred, in his bereavement, has taken pen in hand. We can see him, sitting at his desk down there in the ancient cellar, with all his emblems, souvenirs, and clippings posted up above him and an oblong of gold-and-green brightness shining down through the doorway from the leafy sunshine of the Square. We can see him talking it over with his comrades "the boys"—the State House carpenter and the gardeners, as they sit at their lunch in the cellar. There is the empty saucer, dry and dusty now; in the good old days Fred always brought in a little bottle of milk every morning for Martha. And this is what Fred writes us, word for word:

PHILA Aug 3, 21.

DEAR FRIEND: I thought I would write you a few lines to let you know that I am still at the Hall but the Black cat is gone—without a press agent Martha just became a cat the boys miss her as we had a bag of grass seed the mice got in and they have to hang their lunch on a string but we have a pair of Robbins that sing in the square they would not be long there if Martha was strolling around. We kept one of her kittens when I was on my vacation it was sent to the Morris Refuge with one of the men, on a Friday the next day he got a yellow slip (good bye). Lot of people ask me about her and a Friend of yours left this card: *Dear friend It looks as if Martha is going to have a family—Will you save me two kittens if they are black like their ma!* But she did not have a black kitten so he did not get one.

She left them for a few days came back when they

The Powder of Sympathy

were sent away this was what got her in wrong, but when a fight between two Thomas cats on the lawn was pulled off Martha's doom was sealed. She had the same sleek black coat the same bright eyes but she was in wrong with our Superintendant so I called up and had a boy from the cat home call for her they said it would cost 50 cents so I left the cents and the job of putting her in the basket to one of the men, but her picture is still on the wall.

We are making changes and repairs about the buildings if the tower would interest you would be pleased to take you up when over in Phila had a party from New York up and they said they knew you.

The old janitor lived in the tower because he had to ring the bell for fires funerals and most everything that went on they tell me one son was born there he had three children, the rafter alongside the open fireplace is burned and we found some old shoes worn by children under the floor, and some bones we thought ment a Crime but upon investigation turned out to be soup bones from Sheep Legs. This is about all. Your Friend

FRED ECKERSBERG
Engineer, Independence Hall.

ACCORDING TO HOYLE

"IF IT be true" (remarks old John Mistletoe, in his little known *Life of Edmund Hoyle*) "that a happy life leaves behind it little material for the biographer, and only those whose careers have been marked by the pangs of ambition and the wearinesses of achievement offer maxims for the moralist, then there is little to be said of Edmund Hoyle. And yet it is odd that a man whose name has become proverbial, who lived to the age of close upon a century (1672–1769), and who standardized and codified the chief social amusement of his age into an etiquette which remained unchanged for six generations—it is odd, I say, that this great peaceful benefactor has left so slight a trace in biographical annals. For I ask you, which of Hoyle's contemporaries conferred a more

The Powder of Sympathy

placable and sedentary boon upon the world than
he?"

"Hoyle" (continues Mr. Mistletoe) "was a man of
very speechless humour. It was his wont to say that he
had been lured into the study and metaphysic of whist
because it was a silent game. As is well known, the
game was originally called *whisk;* it was Mr. Hoyle who,
by his continual utterance of the imperative and hush-
ing monosyllable *Whist!* when gaming with those whose
tongues were apt to wag irrelevantly, caused the di-
version, at first only in sport, and then in genuine ear-
nest, to be rechristened. It was a sight not to be for-
gotten, by contemporary account, to see the Master
(as he was known) sitting down at the Three Pigeons
tavern for his afternoon rubber. The mornings he
spent in tutoring wealthy ladies in the rudiments of the
fashionable game, this being the chief source of his
income. He was very particular, moreover, as to the
standing and rank of his pupils; he was much in de-
mand, and could afford to take only such students as
satisfied his fastidious taste for youth and beauty.
In fact, he anticipated the doctrine announced many
years later by John Keats, who remarked, 'I intend
henceforth to have nothing to do with the society of
ladies unless they be handsome. You lose time to no
purpose.'

"It was, I repeat, an agreeable spectacle to witness
the Master driving up to the Three Pigeons about the
hour of (as we would now say) luncheon, in his white
hackney coach with his emblem—the Ace of Hearts—
blazoned on the panel. Before the gaming began he

According to Hoyle

would always take a leisurely meal; indeed, it was his habit to say that no gentleman would ever spend less than three hours at the table. One of his humours was to insist that warm weather was dangerous to his constitution, and that in summer it was desirable to eat sparingly and with deliberation. On days that had, as someone has put it, the humidity of Uriah Heep, this was an example of his menu, which I have found filed in the old papers kept in the vaults of the Three Pigeons:

Service to Mr. Edmund Hoyle, this 28th July 1730, on acct:
  A capon broth, with toasted bread
  A flagon of small ale
  Fricassee of sweetbreads, with currant jelly
  A flask of cool Canary
  Rosted wild ducks, with cheesecake and parsnips
  A jugg of malmsey, from the special butt
  A sallet of shrimpes and candyed cherries
  A hot rabbit pye, with buttered pease and a pottle of mulled claret
  Rhubarbe pasty, with barley wine to ease Mr. Hoyle's digestions
  Plague water for the hott weather

"Having done suitable homage to this judicious nourishment" (Mr. Mistletoe proceeds), "Mr. Hoyle would have brought to him his own yard of clay, which he would leisurely fill with the best pure Virginia leaf, gazing about him the while upon the impatient faces of his friends who were anxious to get to the cards. 'Never indulge the carnal appetites immoderately in hot weather,' he would say, blowing out a long blue whiff into the cool twilight of the old taproom, panelled, in

The Powder of Sympathy

magnificent dark walnut. This was the last word
uttered, for when the Master took his seat at the card
table no man dared speak. A sacred quiet filled the
place as he reached for the pasteboards and deftly cut
for the deal, tossing back his lace cuffs over his lean
yellowish wrists, the colour (he was something bilious)
of old piano keys. The rest was silence, with only the
fall of the cards and the occasional clink of a bottle
when Mr. Hoyle refilled his vase of Burgundy, which
he always drank while gaming. A life of abstemious
control, he said, was needful for one who must keep his
wits alert."

L. E. W.

W E ARE continually obtaining new and piercing glimpses into human life and character. We are now able to assert, without fear of rebuttal, that even men of unblemished intellect and lofty, serene understanding have always some particular point of frailty at which morals, virtue, and integrity collapse in a dark confusion of spiritual wreckage.

Reconsidering the above sentence it seems to need a little clarification. We shall have to explain what we mean, and can only do so by referring, with painful verity, to the Leading Editorial Writer.

L. E. W. came into our kennel yesterday morning and saw lying on our desk a newly published detective novel that a publisher had sent us. "Oh," he said, "What's this?" and began looking it over. We were rather busy at the moment, and paid no particular

The Powder of Sympathy

heed, but looked up a minute later to see him slipping out of our hutch with the book under his arm.

"Here!" we cried, "what are you doing with that book?"

"I'm going to read it," he said, with bland composure.

"Nothing doing," we asserted sternly. "We began to read that in the subway this morning, and we're just getting interested in it. You'll have to wait until we've finished it."

"But you can't read it in the office," he said; "you're too busy."

"So are you," we replied; "but we're going to read it to-night; after an exhausting day we shall need an innocent diversion of that sort."

We did not think of it at the time, but we now remember that there was a curious evasive lustre in his eye. We wish we could make it plain to you how this person, generally a highly cultivated and responsible citizen, occasionally exhibits himself as naïvely unscrupulous, in a way so charming and unashamed that, with lesser men than ourself, he successfully gets away with it.

A little later in the day, again comes L. E. W. into our nook. He looks about in an absent-minded way, giving much the appearance of the *animula vagula blandula* the Roman emperor told about. He made one or two random remarks, and seemed to be pretending that he had intended to say something important but had forgotten what it was. We may say that we penetrated his game immediately. We kept an eye on him, and as soon as he had retired we took

L. E. W.

the detective story and put several newspapers on top of it.

But after all, one cannot sit around the office all day watching the book one is saving for evening reading. By and by we had to go out to lunch, and thought no more of the matter until 5 o'clock. Then, hastily gathering our effects for the trek uptown, we looked for the novel. It was gone.

We could not quite believe it, at first. We thought we must have mislaid it somewhere on top of our desk. We rummaged briskly. No sign of it. With a sudden vile suspicion we ran to L. E. W.'s room. He was gone, too.

Well, we had to console ourself on the ride uptown by reading something else; but you know how it is— when you have set your heart on finishing a particular story. . . .

This morning L. E. W. has just come into our coop, with his usual enigmatic smile, and laid the book before us. We assailed him with bitter reproach and contumely. But we made no impression on him. There is some mysterious knot of villainy in his bosom that leads him to believe that any detective story left within his reach. . . . Of course it is true that writing Leading Editorials for a number of years may well undermine a man's character. But that is what we mean when we say that even men of unblemished intellect and lofty, serene understanding have always some particular point of frailty at which morals, virtue, and integrity collapse in a dark confusion of spiritual wreckage.

The Powder of Sympathy

We haven't mentioned the title of the book, because L. E. W. says it isn't much good. But we are not certain whether that is not just his quaint way of trying to minify the gruesomeness of his offence. It is a perverted form of conscience: he thinks that if he tells us the book is punk we will not regret that our reading was brutally postponed. But we are going to tell him that he missed a trick there. It would have been much more in line with the delightful humour for which he is famous if he had said: "It's a great yarn. You ought to read it."

OUR EXTENSION COURSE

THIS has been a pleasantly serene quiet morning
in the office, and we have been sitting here tenderly
educating ourself by studying the catalogue of Univer-
sity Extension Courses given at Columbia. We may
not have admitted it before, but we are rather ambitious,
and find a great deal in this fasciculus that appeals to
our necessities.

Among the courses we should like to enroll in, first
we come to *Business e163—Personnel methods for office
executives* (Fee $24). This would be highly advanta-
geous to us, to teach us how to get along tactfully with
office boys, proof-readers, leading editorial writers, and
sudden, unexpected telephone calls. We look some-
what wistfully upon *Business e13—Advertising Display
and Mechanics, and Business e17—Salesmanship.* ("The

The Powder of Sympathy

student is given a grounding in the principles of selling
and practice in the presentation of a selling proposition
from its inception in the customer's mind throughout its
development and final consummation as a sale.") But
the course for us, austerely denying ourself the lectures
on *Advanced Advertising Writing*, is *Business e19-20—
Sales promotion* (Fee $24). This "includes a thorough
study of merchandising, direction of a sales force,
methods of breaking down sales resistance." It
specializes in "dealer helps" and regards "consumer
advertising" as only secondary. We agree.

The Graduate Courses in Psychology of Advertising
and Selling we feel are probably too advanced for us.

So we pass eagerly on to literary topics. *English
elf-2f* has an agreeably elvish sound—*Advanced short
story writing;* but it's a bit expensive (Fee $48. We
might not get that much for the story after we had
written it.). *Juvenile story writing* is only $32; but we
elect *English e3f-4f—Play Production.* The fee for that
is only $24, which shows you how much money a lot of
theatrical managers waste; moreover, it is held in the
Attic of Hamilton Hall, which sounds very jolly. The
Attic playwrights were always pretty good. And cer-
tainly we must have *English e11-12—Public speaking,*
which is only $16, and gives us "drill in breathing,
articulation, gesture and reading aloud, after-dinner
speaking; how to stir the emotions and move to action."
Philosophy, of course, must not be neglected: we rather
like the look of *Philosophy e135—Radical, conservative,
and reactionary tendencies in present-day morals,* which
seems to cover the ground. (Fee $24.) *Photoplay*

Our Extension Course

composition e3—Advanced course "deals with the finer phases of character delineation" (Fee $24) and ought to be a pleasant relaxation, for "Scenario editors and directors will address the students from time to time." *Physical education eY1-Y2—Swimming* ($16) will very happily conclude that part of our course.

A great need in our life would obviously be filled by *Secretarial Correspondence e2—Letter writing* (Fee $24). This studies the methods adopted by "Huxley, Lanier, Lowell, Henry James, William James, Mark Twain, Cicero, Pliny the Younger, and the letter writers of the World War" in dealing with their correspondence. But we are anxious to get on to even more congenial subjects. *Cookery e3L—General Principles of cookery and their application. Lectures and laboratory work* (Fee $30) appeals to us. Also *Cookery 41xL—Principles of candy making* ($10) and *Cookery e75L—Large quantity cookery* (Fee $30). The only difficulty here is that the costume required for laboratory courses in cooking is "white cotton clothing, plain skirt; tailored waist; plain white collar; long plain white apron with bib." That presents difficulties.

We thought that we had outlined a very full curriculum for ourself, but then we see that our old friend Professor Roger Loomis is giving a course (*English eB10*) on *Argumentative writing*, "planned especially for those interested in the writing of editorials and controversial articles." That certainly we must also have (Fee $24).

The total seems to be $270, and certainly the excitement sounds well worth it.

SOME RECIPES

I. MULLED CIDER

ON A clear, cold afternoon towards the end of October go to the Cider Mill at Jericho, Long Island, and obtain a gallon jug of cider.

Take this home and put in a cool place in the cellar, away from observation. Cider is rather a bold and forward beverage: ever since Eden was first established in an apple orchard the fruit has been tainted with a secret capsule of sin: it is well to let the jug work (in the fine old brewmaster's sense of that word) in private, where its conduct need not be a source of scandal.

Drive the cork in as tightly as possible; but, since Man is no match for Nature, it will not be possible to prevent its extrusion. The best way to deal with this problem is to keep chained in the cellar a trained Cider Hound, a breed of dog known only on the North Shore of Long Island. This is an animal which, by long instruction, has been taught to howl when he hears the whoop of a cider cork blown out by accumulating gases. When the dog howls hasten to the cellar, restopper the jug, fondle the animal, and give

Some Recipes

him a small piece of Roquefort cheese to keep him keen.

Continue this process until the cider has worked for five days—not longer, or you may (like Faust) unchain dark forces with which you cannot cope. At the end of the Fifth Day release the animal and carry the jug upstairs.

Late that night, after the family has retired, pour a pint of cider into a saucepan and heat it—preferably over the glowing logs of a wood fire—until it steams. Then stir in three tablespoons of granulated sugar. Do not be startled by the violence of the foaming and hissing that ensues—this is only Nature at her inscrutable tasks of making life puzzling for dogmatists.

Into the steaming sweetened cider pour as much brandy from the family medicine chest as you think you can spare. If brandy is not obtainable, whiskey will serve. If whiskey is not obtainable, invite some friend who has recently made a transatlantic voyage and ask him to breathe gently upon the saucepan while it is heating.

Serve the beverage hot, and, while drinking, utter any toast or sentiment that is a favourite in your family. Reckon quantities at the rate of not more than one pint per person. Mulled cider is recommended during years of coal shortage, when the house may be chilly; but it is not to be trifled with save by the most hardy.

Before retiring walk three times round the house and try to name all the constellations. If you don't know the names, give them new ones. This quiets the pulse.

(*P. S.—This is an old recipe, swallowed down through*

The Powder of Sympathy

*several generations, which accounts for some of its ana-
chronisms.)*

II. STEWED RHUBARB

Early in the spring buy a rhubarb root on Vesey
Street. The root itself, an uncouth, gnarled object, is
not beautiful, but it bears small red and yellow shoots
that are highly decorative, like little Spanish flags.

This root must be planted in a churchyard, prefer-
ably Episcopalian, which gives the rhubarb a pleasantly
Athanasian flavour, much esteemed by connoisseurs.
We specially recommend St. Paul's churchyard, partly
because the high buildings round about keep the sharp
winds of early spring away from the tender sprouts,
but also because the pleasant hum of young women
reading Keable and Ruby M. Ayres aloud at lunch
time on the benches encourages the plant and hastens
its growth.

The stalks must not be picked prematurely. Wait
until they are a brilliant red. The best way to get this
right is to test them with a leather-bound copy of one
of Kipling's books, in that scarlet leather edition. When
the stalks are exactly the same colour as *Stalky & Co.*,
pick them.

Take them home, wash them, cut them into cylin-
drical lengths, and have them stewed in the usual
manner.

III. HAGGIS AND BAGPIPES

Haggis should always be served with bagpipes. The
reason for this will be explained later.

Some Recipes

In our recipes we always try to give the easiest way in which our favourite dishes may be attained. The easiest way to enjoy Haggis is to enlist the assistance of a number of Scotsmen, who by tradition, training, temperament, and centuries of romantic strife have fitted themselves to prepare and eat this sovereign piece of resistance.

Make friends, therefore, with as many prominent local Scots as possible. Season the mixture by adding a few directors of some well-known Scottish steamship companies. These friendships must be cultivated gently and cannot be unduly hurried. Subscribe to the *Caledonian* or some other Scottish-American magazine. Eventually, if all goes well, you may be invited to a dinner of the Caledonian Club or the St. Andrews Society, or a luncheon on an Anchor Line steamship. At this dinner The Haggis will be served.

The bagpipes are for the purpose of muffling any metaphysical argument that may arise round the tables, and also to drown out any stories that begin "There was a man frae Aberdeen——"

Do not ask your neighbour at table why it is that the pipes always play the same tune. If you do, you will not be invited again. It is better to garnish the occasion with a few carefully chosen Scottish phrases —such as *'Tis a braw day the day; I'll no can keep that appointment for three o'clock; Let the warld gang tapsalteerie; Whaur's Wullie Shaksper noo?*

ADVENTURES OF A CURRICULAR ENGINEER

HAVING made up our mind to become an engineer, we thought it would be a mistake not to take advantage of all possible aid. We were passing the corner of Church and Fulton streets just now when we saw, in a drugstore, a fair young lady sitting in the window conducting a demonstration of Violet Rays. She wore a most appealing expression, held in her hand a glass tube with a bulbous end which was filled with pale blue electrical excitement, and was displaying various placards inviting the public to enjoy a free treatment of the Violet Ray. This Ray, her placards said, confers all imaginable pleasures and animations upon the user, It subdues inflammations and tumescences; it imparts the vigorous glow of health and beauty; it dispels

Adventures of a Curricular Engineer

lethargy and that Omar Khayyám kind of feeling that we get on a warm day in spring; it confers (so we gathered) all the benefits of Pelmanism without having to read George Creel's little essays.

A large crowd of loitering gentry stood at the window watching the lady who was applying the Violet Ray to her own person and getting more seemly every moment. But none of them, self-satisfied chaps apparently, seemed eager to try the effect of the sparks when she pushed them towards the pane. But we, in our humility, feeling the need of greater ambition and resoluteness, offered our hand to the thunder-stone and absorbed as much of the life-giving current as she was willing to give away. We felt sure, somehow, that the Violet Ray would help us in learning to understand our new self-propelled vehicle. (We have to call it that, for to call it a *car* is a little too imposing; and to call it a flivver is a little too degraded; besides, it isn't. Hereafter we shall call her by her given name, which is Dame Quickly.)

Our first adventures with Dame Quickly, by the way, were not devoid of excitement. One who, on his second day as a curricular engineer, navigates the main roads of Long Island on Decoration Day may be said to be a daring soul. Titania, who was with us, says that our publisher passed by in his limousine and looked annoyed because we did not acknowledge his friendly gesture; but, indeed, all the concentrated powers of our retinal system were focussed upon the highway, and even if he docks our royalties for rudeness we cannot help it. We noticed, however, that the drivers who

overhauled us as we prowled cautiously along had a way
of looking sideways at us in a fixed, not exactly hostile,
but at any rate curious gaze, as though to reassure them-
selves as to what kind of person this was. We remained
bland and undismayed, for we are still a driver without
spirit; we will give any man as much of the road as he
wants; we have no sense of humiliation, nor any com-
petitive lust. Any collisions that Dame Quickly suffers
will occur only in her rearward parts.

Oyster Bay, we aver, is a dangerous place to be on
the afternoon of Decoration Day. We reached that
amiable town around two hours post meridiem, exceed-
ingly hungry from our anxieties en route. As we un-
obtrusively trundled along the main street our general
nervousness was not allayed by the spectacle of a motor
fire engine rushing towards us at full speed. Our
general idea was to attract as little attention as possible,
so we made a bashful détour among back ways. To
our horror, there was another fire engine, also roaring
along at a furious pace. The whole town of Oyster
Bay is burning up, was our thought; however, that is a
small matter compared to getting this vehicle to a safe
place where we can eat lunch and at the same time
watch her with a paternal eye. (Our neighbour in
Salamis had said something about new cars getting
stolen, and we had a dreadful vision of being trailed
along the highways by an experienced crook who would
get away with Dame Quickly if we left her unwatched
for five minutes.) But every time we approached the
main street, trying to slip in unobserved, either a man
on a motor bike would rush up and shout something

quite unintelligible or else we would hear the roar of another fire engine dashing about. Gradually we divined that a number of Long Island fire departments were having their annual competition; but the fact that it was only a game, and not a real fire, made things worse. No fire engine would go to a real fire with the furious zest with which those fellows sped up and down the street. So, chivvied about by fire engines and cops, we had to take lunch at the only place we could approach unobserved, a very small hash-house which, since we cannot praise, we will not mention.

However, we had cause, later, to be grateful to these fire engines that had so terrified us. For, after some delightful rambling by blue watersides and under green colonnades of ancient trees, we found ourselves endeavouring to shake off the pursuing traffic on a remote and hilly byroad. We shall not go into the why and how of this matter, but the fact is that at one moment the honourable and shining Dame Quickly might have been seen docilely purring along the road; and then, a few minutes later, she was insecurely suspended half over the slope of a steep ravine, quite immovable. The curricular engineer wrung his hands. This, he asserted, is the End. With beaded brow he made some amateurish play with logs of wood that he found in that solitary woodland; but the back wheels of the beautiful, the lovely, the spirited Dame Quickly only revolved grindingly in the sand, and her commodious form hung inert, not to say in peril. Then did the engineer realize that, even on such short acquaintance, he loved her already; and the thought of intrusting her sweet body to

[85]

The Powder of Sympathy

the harsh hands of an alien garage man was poisonous.
And if we leave her to go back to a garage, we thought,
the earth will give; she will plunge to her doom. Ti-
tania, we think, prayed.

And then, gods from the machine, here came the Glen
Cove Fire Department, some twenty strong, merrily
speeding past. What they were doing up this bosky by-
path we did not halt to inquire. The hand of Provi-
dence, patently, was at work. When the hand of
Providence appears, one does not stop to inquire into its
palmistry. We laid, bashfully, our case before these
great-hearted lads. With a shout they seized our dear
Mrs. Quickly; strong arms and gallant hearts of Glen
Cove bore her up the perilous precipice; she stood
again on level roadway, catching the sun on her noble
enamel. The task accomplished, the Glen Cove Fire
Department, with their two red engines behind them,
looked humorously at us and seemed tacitly to inquire
how any sane man would get into such a position. We
said, sheepishly, a word of explanation. They roared
with laughter.

SANTAYANA IN THE SUBWAY

TO CONFESS one's self to have had a seizure of
pure happiness is, by one theory, to admit one's self
a boob.

And yet we do not know when we have been more
happy—in our own secret definition of that state—
than when we set off for the subway yesterday noon-
time. A more timid or more subtle spirit, perhaps,
would not dare the envy of the gods by mentioning it.
A fig for the gods!

For, in the first place, that clear pearly light, the
patchwork of sun and shadow down the harsh channel
of Broadway, the close embrace of wintry air (so dart-
ingly cold that it seemed to enfold and surround one
as water does the bather) and the great Singer tower

[87]

The Powder of Sympathy

lifting above the cliffs in a tender wash of blue—these were enough of themselves to make one lively. Again, we were bound uptown on an errand of pure generosity, to turn over to a publisher the MS. of a book written by a friend of ours, which we believe to be a fine book. Further, we even considered it possible that the publisher might buy our lunch.

We went down into the subway, and clanked through the turnstile. The thought occurred to us that it seems pretty poor sportsmanship to make merry—as some of the papers have been doing—over the fact that many people have devised ways of bilking the turnstiles. We suppose we shall be accused of having been bought with mickle gold, but we must admit that we have never had any hankering to cheat the subway. There are many corporations we would cheat without a qualm, but the subway is not one of them. It gives us more for a nickel—not only in the way of transportation, but also privacy, mental relaxation, and scrutiny of the human scene—than anything else we know.

We stood in the subway express, about to open a book. We noticed, sitting a little farther along, a young woman whose hat interested us. It was pierced in front by a pin of silver and brilliants, zigzag in shape, representing (we supposed) a bolt of lightning. It was emblematic, we opined, of high-spirited humanity itself, that toys with lightning in more ways than one. This of itself, while valuable for meditation, was not the cause of our happiness. We had a book with us, a book that we have wanted to read for some time. We began to read it.

Santayana in the Subway

It was not necessary to travel more than a few lines to be perfectly happy. Why were we happy? We could write many pages to try to explain it to you, and even then should probably fail. This is what we read:

About the middle of the nineteenth century, in the quiet sunshine of provincial prosperity, New England had an Indian summer of the mind; and an agreeable reflective literature showed how brilliant that russet and yellow season could be. There were poets, historians, orators, preachers, most of whom had studied foreign literatures and had travelled; they demurely kept up with the times; they were universal humanists. But it was all a harvest of leaves; these worthies had an expurgated and barren conception of life; theirs was the purity of sweet old age. Sometimes they made attempts to rejuvenate their minds by broaching native subjects; they wished to prove how much matter for poetry the new world supplied, and they wrote "Rip van Winkle," "Hia——"

That was exactly the first page, as we read it; we needed to go no further to have cause for complete and unblemished satisfaction. There was the kind of writing that we understand, that speaks to us. There, barring the fact that Rip was not written in New England, was that exact, humorous, and telling use of every word—"*demurely* kept up with the times"; "the purity of sweet old age"—if you don't get pleasure out of that sort of thing, then there is no use trying to labour it in. And there, in every line and syllable, was exactly what we had expected to find—a genuine Intellect speaking, and not a pseudo and jejuvenile "Young Intellectual." There were urbanity, charm, the word well-weighed, the

[89]

strong, reticulated thought. To go into private minutiæ, we even had additional pleasure from the fact that the usage of the semicolons (a matter of great delight to some enthusiasts) conformed to our own private sense of felicity. And we gazed about the car in a tranquil ecstasy.

The book was George Santayana's *Character and Opinion in the United States*.

We said to ourself, in a kind of anger (for truly a certain ingredient of anger is necessary for complete happiness; a zealous espousal of what one believes to be worth while carries with it the most cheerful flush of irritation towards those who have not, one thinks, sufficiently espoused it)—we said, Why is it that no one has hitherto driven in upon our mind that this book (published a year ago) is one that we could not possibly get along without? Why is it that our admirable colleague L. E. W., from whom we borrowed it, did not long ago come and sit on our desk and talk to us, endlessly, calmly, suasively, about it and about?

We went on reading, and stood there in as perfectly felicitous an absorption as we have ever enjoyed. We could have said to that golden instant, as Mephistopheles promised Faust he would be able to say, "Verweile doch, du bist so schön!" We had committed Grand Larceny. We had achieved what the news headlines daily describe as a "Daring Robbery." We had stolen, from uncajolable and endless Time, a Perfect Moment.

We see you smile gravely, and perhaps pityingly, at our simplicity. Never mind. We shall never forget the mood of serene peacefulness and cheer in which

Santayana in the Subway

we then turned to Mr. Santayana's preface and began to read:

Civilization is perhaps approaching one of those long winters that overtake it from time to time. Romantic Christendom—picturesque, passionate, unhappy episode—may be coming to an end. Such a catastrophe would be no reason for despair. . . .

Ah, we said to ourself, that is the kind of writing that makes us truly happy!

We cannot remember when we have marvelled more truly at the pregnancy, the wit, and the exquisite underpiercing insight of any book. We should like to ask those competent to speak—certainly we ourself are not competent; and it is the sheerest bumptiousness for us even to offer an opinion on a book so consummately wise and lovely—whether there has ever been written any more thrillingly potent examination of a whole civilization? In a book so packed and rifted with gold one knows not where to start quoting; but almost at random we seize this passage—not by any means one of the subtlest, but it will serve to begin with:

. . . The American is imaginative; for where life is intense, imagination is intense also. Were he not imaginative he would not live so much in the future. But his imagination is practical, and the future it forecasts is immediate; it works with the clearest and least ambiguous terms known to his experience, in terms of number, measure, contrivance, economy, and speed. He is an idealist working on matter. Understanding as

[91]

The Powder of Sympathy

he does the material potentialities of things, he is successful in invention, conservative in reform, and quick in emergencies. All his life he jumps into the train after it has started and jumps out before it has stopped; and he never once gets left behind, or breaks a leg.

Or, if you prefer, consider this:

That philosophers should be professors is an accident, and almost an anomaly. Free reflection about everything is a habit to be imitated, but not a subject to expound; and an original system, if the philosopher has one, is something dark, perilous, untested, and not ripe to be taught, nor is there much danger that any one will learn it. The genuine philosopher—as Royce liked to say, quoting the Upanishads—wanders alone like the rhinoceros. . . . If philosophers must earn their living and not beg (which some of them have thought more consonant with their vocation), it would be safer for them to polish lenses like Spinoza, or to sit in a black skull-cap and white beard at the door of some unfrequented museum, selling the catalogues and taking in the umbrellas; these innocent ways of earning their breadcard in the future republic would not prejudice their meditations and would keep their eyes fixed, without undue affection, on a characteristic bit of that real world which it is their business to understand. . . . At best, the true philosopher can fulfil his mission very imperfectly, which is to pilot himself or at most a few voluntary companions who may find themselves in the same boat. It is not easy for him to shout, or address a crowd; he must be silent for long seasons; for he is watching stars that move slowly and in courses that it is possible though difficult to foresee, and he is crushing all things in his heart as a winepress until his life and their secret flow out together.

[92]

Santayana in the Subway

You understand (don't you?) that we do not necessarily recommend Santayana for *you*. As we grow, painfully, in sagacity, we realize the absurdity of recommending anything to anybody. We are simply saying that for us he fulfils (both in what we agree with and what we dissent from) most of the requirements of our private conception of beauty and happiness.

It is a book that quickens the mind. Continuing it on the train, as the smoking car spins through those green Long Island meadows, we look round on our fellow travellers with renewed amazement. Somehow it gives us a strange pleasure to see them immersed in the *Evening Journal* or the *Evening World*, those grotesque monuments of human frailty. How damnable it would be if they were all reading Santayana. How we should hate them! We know that all humanity are precious fools, and ourself the most arrant of the lot; but we like them that way. It adds to the cheerful comedy of the scene.

Certainly you would have said that two names that sound something alike are at opposite ends of the intellectual spectrum—Santayana and Pollyanna. And yet, oddly enough, the thought has come to us that the foundations of the two philosophies interlock. Santayana's method of extracting happiness from life; his perfection of cool, tender, smiling, grave, cruel, and imperturbable resignation; the exquisitely sophisticated contentment of his solitude, flight from needless buzbuz, reverie in places haunted by old association; his noble ridicule of destiny—all this brings to a reasonably sophisticated mind the same kind of heavenly

[93]

The Powder of Sympathy

refreshment and sense of truth that simpler people find in literature of the Pollyanna sort.

We vented this tentative idea to some colleagues of ours, and they leapt upon us with shouts of anger and contradiction.

Yet we think there is something in it. There is no way of assessing the operations of other people's minds. But we are inclined to think that very possibly the pure happiness we experience in Mr. Santayana's calm, humorous, disillusioned, and poetic reveries is not essentially different from the cheerful exaltation some young woman feels reading either of the Mrs. Porters in the Y. W. C. A.

MADONNA OF THE TAXIS

SPEAKING of commuting, the Long Island Railroad owes us $7, and we are wondering how long it will take us to collect it.

The incident, tragic as it was, will prove a lesson to us never again to be unfaithful to our beloved Brooklyn.

On Wednesday evening we had to decide whether we would take the train for Salamis from the Penn. Station or from Brooklyn. We decided we would take it from Penn. Station, because we were without reading matter, and knew that at Penn. Station we could stop in at the bookshop in the Arcade and get something to amuse us en route. All began merrily. We got to the station at 9 o'clock, bought an Everyman edition of Kit Marlowe's plays, and, well supplied with tobacco, we set sail on the 9:10 vehicle. How excellent are the resources of civilization, said we to ourself, as we retraced

The Powder of Sympathy

the sorrows of Dr. Faustus. Here we are, we cried,
sitting at ease in a brilliantly lighted smoker reading
"Cut is the branch that might have grown full straight,"
and in fifty minutes we will greet again the shabby but
well-loved station at Salamis. We even meditated
writing a little verse in Marlowe's own vein, to be called
"The Passionate Long Islander to His Love":

> Come live with me and be my love
> And we will all the pleasures prove
> That Patchogue, Speonk, Hempstead fields,
> Ronkonkoma or Yaphank yields.

At this moment, which was 9:15, and just issuing
from the tunnel, the train stopped, all lights went out,
and we sat gazing at the dreary dormitory of Pullman
cars in Long Island City.

For thirty-six minutes we sat so. Occasionally there
would be the sound of a heavy sigh, a long-drawn sus-
piration of some mentally troubled commuter whose
feels (in the language of Opal Whiteley) were not satis-
faction feels; but commuters are a tested and toughened
lot. The time lagged heavily and darkly by, but there
was no shrill outcry, no futile beating of the breast.
One shining thought there was to console, and the con-
ductor ratified it (we asked him ourself). "Oh, yes,"
he said, "the Oyster Bay connection waits for this train
at Jamaica." We envisaged the picture of that bat-
tered and faithful old Oyster Bay loco, waiting patiently
for its lovers along the windy platform, and we were
heartened.

Madonna of the Taxis

But when we got to Jamaica, the old harridan steam train had gone.

Then, indeed, hearts were broken. Then there was scudding to and fro, and voices raised in menace and imprecation. The next train to Oyster Bay, said the officials, leaves at 12:10. The mourners gathered in little groups, drawn by their several affinities. Those who yearned for Garden City formed one posse. Those who yearned for Babylon and Bayshore, another. But, let it proudly be said, the Oyster Bay group were the loudest in outcry, the angriest in mood. We have a pride of our own on the Oyster Bay branch. ("Cut was the branch that might have gone full straight.") In Salamis alone, Gen. Pershing is living there, and Dorothy Gish visits sometimes. Are we to be trifled with? Off went the Oyster Bay contingent, some twenty angry, to see the Station Master. Words were passed, without avail.

We ourself are a realist at such moments. We saw that the Station Master held no balm for the sufferers. We fled from the brutal scene. Downstairs one taxi, the only one, was just embarking a passenger and wheeling off. For an instant (we confess it) our nerve was shaken. We screamed, and there was in that scream the dreadful keening note of a lioness balked of her whelps or a commuter ravished of his train. Ha! the taxi halted. It was, strangely enough, a lady chauffeur, and tender of heart. No man chauffeur would have halted at such a time, but this madonna of taxi drivers had a bosom of pity. Her fare, already in situ, was bound for Garden City. They agreed to take us along,

The Powder of Sympathy

and after Garden City had been made she would steer for Salamis.

O Lady Taxi Driver of Jamaica, a benison befall thee. The wind roared stiffly across the plains, and the small henry made leeway. The small henry scuttled like a dog, half sideways, nosing several points upward into the gale in order to pursue a straight course. The other passenger was plainly a Man of Large Affairs, sunk in a generous melancholy. There was little talk. We sat, or, when the roadway required it, leaped aloft like striking trout. Garden City was duly reached, and then, by and by, the woody glens of Salamis Heights. The fare we paid our saviour was $7. We did not grudge it her. She has a seven-year-old boy, and all day she keeps house, all night she runs her taxi. But, in candour, we think the railroad owes us that $7. It has ever been held a point of honour that the Oyster Bay train shall wait for its children. When there are only two after-dinner trains, that seems not much to ask.

If we had gone from Brooklyn, all would have been well.

MATTHEW ARNOLD AND EXODONTIA

I

THIS year (1922) brings the centennial of Matthew
Arnold's birth. Except for a few of his more im-
portant poems, we confess to an affectionate ignorance
about Arnold. Of course, we remember taking notes
during a number of lectures about him when we were at
college; a few catchwords about culture and anarchy;
sweetness and light; seeing life steadily and seeing it
whole; Barbarians, Philistines, and Populace—a few
faded buntings of this sort flutter rather dingily from
the halliards of our memory; and we remember that he
had exceptionally fine whiskers. We used to speculate,

The Powder of Sympathy

in the jejune manner of youth, as to whether Matt, as Rugby boy and Oxford undergraduate, was not a rather amusing contrast to the robust Tom Brown whom his father made famous. But, as you will see, Arnold has never been more than an interesting and gracious wraith in our mind. Those of his essays that we were told to reread we have forgotten, or else (more likely) we never opened.

But rambling not long ago in the cellar of Mr. Mendoza's bookshop on Ann Street we found, with a shock of excitement, a little book published in Boston in 1888, called *Civilization in the United States: First and Last Impressions of America*, by Matthew Arnold. We wondered whether this little book had ever been perused by any of the vigorous skeptics who published a recent large volume with the same title. They made, as far as we can recall, no allusion to it. Yet they would have found in it much nourishing meat.

Matthew Arnold's analysis of American life is interesting to read now. Much of his estimate he would certainly wish to revise. We forget just when it was that he travelled over here—in the 80's, we suppose—but his general comment was that American civilization was not *interesting*. He used the word in a very special sense, apparently; he explains it by mentioning the sense of beauty and the sense of distinction. He found American life lacking in charm and in those elements of beauty which appeal to the tranquil and more reflective emotions. It is entertaining—in view of later developments—to hear him say that "the American cities have hardly anything to please a trained or a natural

Matthew Arnold and Exodontia

sense for beauty . . . where the Americans succeed
best in their architecture—in that art so indicative and
educative of a people's sense for beauty—is in the fash-
ion of their villa-cottages in wood." One cannot help
putting a little covey of exclamation marks in the mar-
gin at that point. Those "villa-cottages in wood" of
the 1880's are now the jest and rapidly vanishing pox
of our suburbs. Even to Abraham Lincoln, by the way,
he denies "distinction." He says, "shrewd, sagacious,
humorous, honest, courageous, firm; a man with qual-
ities deserving the most sincere esteem and praise, but
he has not distinction." We have read somewhere (it
is an unforgettable crumb of human oddity) that Arnold
was chiefly interested in Lincoln's assassination because
the murderer shouted in Latin as he leapt on the stage.

There is much that might be said about a point of
view so sincere, so sympathetic, so bravely honest, and
yet so lacking in some qualities of imagination as that
we seem to find in Arnold's book. But what we want
to quote is a portion of his comment on the American
newspapers. Perhaps it is more nearly true still—and,
since Northcliffe, more nearly true of British newspapers
also—than any other part of his remarks. But we wish
to quote it without either assent or denial. He wrote:

You must have lived amongst their newspapers to
know what they are. If I relate some of my own ex-
periences, it is because these will give a clear enough
notion of what the newspapers over there are, and one
remembers more definitely what has happened to one-
self. Soon after arriving in Boston I opened a Boston
newspaper and came upon a column headed: "Tick-

The Powder of Sympathy

ings." By *tickings* we are to understand news conveyed through the tickings of the telegraph. The first "ticking" was: "Matthew Arnold is sixty-two years old"—an age, I must just say in passing, which I had not then reached. The second "ticking" was: "Wales says, Mary is a darling"; the meaning being that the Prince of Wales expressed great admiration for Miss Mary Anderson. This was at Boston, the American Athens. I proceeded to Chicago. An evening paper was given me soon after I arrived; I opened it, and found under a large-type heading, "*We have seen him arrive*," the following picture of myself: "He has harsh features, supercilious manners, parts his hair down the middle, wears a single eyeglass and ill-fitting clothes." Notwithstanding this rather unfavourable introduction, I was most kindly and hospitably received at Chicago. It happened that I had a letter for Mr. Medill, an elderly gentleman of Scotch descent, the editor of the chief newspaper in those parts, the Chicago *Tribune*. I called on him, and we conversed amicably together. Some time afterwards, when I had gone back to England, a New York paper published a criticism of Chicago and its people, purporting to have been contributed by me to the *Pall Mall Gazette* over here. It was a poor hoax, but many people were taken in and were excusably angry, Mr. Medill of the Chicago *Tribune* amongst the number. A friend telegraphed to me to know if I had written the criticism. I, of course, instantly telegraphed back that I had not written a syllable of it. Then a Chicago paper is sent to me; and what I have the pleasure of reading, as the result of my contradiction, is this: "Arnold denies; Mr. Medill refuses to accept Arnold's disclaimer; says Arnold is a cur."

There were California boosters even then, we note. Arnold quotes a Coast newspaper which called all East-

[102]

Matthew Arnold and Exodontia

erners "the unhappy denizens of a forbidding clime,"
and added: "The time will surely come when all roads
will lead to California. Here will be the home of art,
science, literature, and profound knowledge."

II

You probably thought (and justly) that we cut off
Matthew Arnold rather abruptly yesterday. Well, we
did; but there's always a reason for everything. We
had to hurry uptown, by order of Dr. James Kendall
Burgess, the philosophical dentist, to call on Dr. Hillel
Feldman for some exodontia. In the old days, we dare
say, it would have been called having a tooth pulled,
but we like the word exodontia much better.

Now, since we have always been candid with our
clients, we will admit that we were a bit nervous. Of
course, we knew that these operations rarely turn out
fatally; but still, we could see, as soon as we got into
that medical office building at 616 Madison Avenue,
that we were out of our element. Everywhere there
were trained nurses in uniform—going about on "er-
rands of mercy," we supposed. There was one near the
elevator downstairs; there was another in the corridor
upstairs; and the soothing, tender way they asked
what we wanted made us, somehow, even more con-
scious of the painful nature of our errand.

However, another of our habits came somewhat to
our rescue when we found ourself sitting in Dr. Feld-
man's chair. We are timid, we admit; but we are also
inquisitive and like to know the details of what's going
on. We could see right away that Dr. Feldman is a

The Powder of Sympathy

tactful man, for he keeps his instruments under a neat little napkin so that you don't have a chance to be alarmed by all those interesting gouges and pincers. Dr. Feldman immediately pierced our jaw with some stuff he called novocaine, and then, quite as though this was a very commonplace proceeding, began to chat leisurely. "You know," he said, "a fellow can't read your things in the paper just for a laugh. Those other fellows' columns, you can read them and get some fun out of it; but your stuff, you have to read carefully and wade through a long slab to see what it's all about."

"Yes," we said, "we're like you, Doctor. We believe in giving our patients discipline—making them suffer."

Now, of course, we said this hoping to give Dr. Feldman a chance to say right away, "Oh, I'm not going to make you suffer. This won't hurt a bit."

He didn't say it, however. He chuckled in a way that seemed to us a trifle threatening. We hastened to appease him by saying some complimentary things about his shining, complicated apparatuses. To our displeasure we found that our jaw now had a numb and frozen feeling, so that we could not talk properly. We could only mumble.

The calm, genial way in which Dr. Feldman sized us up as we sat there with our jaw getting more and more queer—a curious sensation of mingled freezing and heat —reassured us a little. "Does the novocaine make perspiration come out on your forehead like that?" he asked, with a sort of intellectual curiosity. "No, no," we hastened to say, out of the other side of our mouth.

Matthew Arnold and Exodontia

"We've been hurrying to get here, Doctor. Didn't
want to keep you waiting." That was true; but we
were afraid he would think we were scared. He began
to toy gently with the corner of the napkin on his instru-
ment stand. We were tremendously eager to see what
kind of tools he had concealed there. But he out-
witted us. He suddenly uttered the excellent words we
had been hoping for. "This'll be absolutely painless,"
he said, and then with great gusto and alacrity he
sprang upon us. There was a sound rather like grind-
ing out a stone that is imbedded in a frozen pond. It
was very interesting. We think the adverb *absolutely*
perhaps was a trifle too strong: perhaps a precisian in
words might substitute *almost;* but at any rate our sense
of excitement far outweighed any small twinges. By the
time we thought that he was getting well started,
"That's all," he said. "Perhaps you'd better have a
little stimulant."

Well, naturally, by this time we felt that Dr. Feldman
was one of the best friends we had ever had. We
shook his hand warmly and assured him we wouldn't
have missed the adventure for anything. Then we
went to browse for a few minutes in the second-hand
bookshops on Fifty-ninth Street to think it over. We
called on Mr. Mitchell Kennerley at the Anderson
Galleries. As our jaw was still very much frostbitten,
we couldn't talk very clearly, and we had to hold our
pipe in an unaccustomed corner of our mouth. We fear
he misunderstood our condition; but he was too polite
to say so. Our mind went back to Matthew Arnold.

Matthew Arnold, as we were saying, complained that

[105]

The Powder of Sympathy

American civilization was not *interesting*. A silly thing to say, it seems to us. He meant, evidently, that it did not supply the kind of interest to which he was accustomed, or for which he yearned. For surely, to any one ready to lay aside preconceptions, *interesting* is exactly what American life has always been. We reflected that the one word we instinctively used in explaining to Dr. Feldman how we had enjoyed our visit to him was just that—*interesting*. We feel that if Arnold had been a little more courageously imaginative he might have felt the same way about America. It may very truly have troubled some of his sensitive nerves; it may have caused him terror and shuddering; it may have seemed violent and tragic; but surely he might have seen that it was a teeming laboratory of life and amazement. We believe, by the way, that it was 1883 when he was first here; for we have just noticed in Mendoza's bookshop a copy of Arnold's poems autographed by him for a lady, and dated 1883. It was an American edition, so probably he signed it while in this country.

Mr. Arnold's comments on American newspapers, we should like to add, were perhaps just a little scarce in humour. It is all very well to stand aghast at the jocular irreverence of much newspaper writing; but evidently it never occurred to Arnold that much of it is not mere vulgarity but expresses a national sense of gusto and hilarity that is far from a bad thing.

We cannot resist concluding this too brief excursus by quoting a letter which came to us from a mysterious correspondent—whom we know only by the initials

Matthew Arnold and Exodontia

N. O. N. P.   It seems to us the most charming portrait
of Arnold that we have ever seen.   N. O. N. P. wrote:

There is no art to read the mind's construction in the
face; but it is possible to see the correspondence, after
the cypher has been well de-coded.   Matthew Arnold—
a plain face—a plain brow—dark hair, parted exactly
in the middle—and cheek whiskers!   A long nose,
slightly thick, and drooping—a wide plaster of mouth,
firm but highly sensitive—a six-foot stature and slim
build—a scholastic figure and face and cut—tutorial,
perhaps; and in that plain face the expression of *impres-
sion*—that is, the visible result of sensitiveness.   Every
pre-natal and post-natal fineness of his rarely fine, high,
sincere mind pervaded the texture of his countenance
and gave its stamp of authentic quality to render
nugatory anything that might seem superficially to
counteract the inherent integrity.   Superficially, it
might have seemed (perhaps) a smug face or a super-
cilious one; not inwardly.   Inward daintiness might
have been there, as there certainly was fastidiousness,
if not a frigidity.   But a warm heart corresponded to
that mouth, which was thick without seeming sensual,
and back of that face was a just, a clear, a steady mind,
a heat for right and truth, a manly spirit with a manly
intellect, a manly sense of clean beauty—and with
whatever æsthetic narrowings (if they existed), a
broad, direct, noble simplicity and humanity.   I hope
he will verily have his reward, for in his brave, unwhin-
ing, spotless life, he did most valuable, intelligent drud-
gery for his bread; and out of a beautiful gift composed
the loftiest, simplest, broadest, gravest, most reserved
and felt, and perhaps most musical and moving poem
(as pure poem) of his generation—*Sohrab and Rustum*.
It lacks all the prettinesses of his contemporaries, but is
the sole product of his time, in "The Grand Style"—

this, however, being of course only the individual opinion of the present commenter.

If a man, one hundred years after his birth, still evokes such graceful and pensive homage, he has evidently some durable claim upon our hearts. Ever since our teens we have wondered what *Sohrab and Rustum* was about and why it was always assigned as required study for College Entrance. Now we intend to read it.

DAME QUICKLY AND THE BOILROASTER

SOMETHING had happened to Dame Quickly's storage battery, and all the amperes seemed to have escaped. An extremely friendly and cheerful young man came up from Fred Seaman's garage, with mysterious medical-looking instruments, to grant a consultation. In the course of the chat he remarked, "If you once ride in a *Boilroaster* car, you'll never be satisfied with any other."

His energetic hands were at that moment deep in our loved Dame Quickly's mechanisms; she was wholly at his mercy; naturally we did not feel like contradicting him or saying anything tactless. We wondered, but only privately, whether the fact that Fred Seaman is the local agent for the *Boilroaster* had anything to do with this comment? Or perhaps, we thought to ourself, our friend the battery expert really is a convinced enthusiast for the *Boilroaster*, and felt that way about it before he took a job at Fred Seaman's establishment? We were sorry that William James was dead, for we

The Powder of Sympathy

felt that the author of *The Will to Believe* would be the man to whom to submit this philosophical problem. We were puzzled, because only a few days earlier another man had said to us (with an equal accent of decisiveness and conviction) that he would rather have a Dame Quickly than any *Boilroaster* ever made. "They stand up better than any of 'em," he had said. Suddenly it occurred to us how useful it would be if there were some kind of spiritual gauge—like the hydrometer our friend was plunging into the cells of the Dame's battery—which one could dip into a man's mind to test the intellectual mixture of his remarks; to evaluate the proportions of those various liquids (the strong acid of self-interest, the mild distilled water of candour, etc.) which electrify his mental ignition.

Well, how about the *Boilroaster*, we said—(searching for a technical term that would show him we are a practical man)—Do they stand up?

He suggested that we get into his own *Boilroaster*, which stood grandly overshining the dusty Dame (reminding us of those pictures where a silhouette of the new *Majestic* is placed behind a little picture of the *Teutonic* or some other humble ship of older days) and take a run around Salamis while he tinkered with the battery.

Oh, no, we said nervously. Dame Quickly is the only car we know how to run, and besides the gear shift is different in the *Boilroaster;* we might get confused and have to come all the way home in reverse, which would be bad for our reputation in the village.

Have you ever ridden in the *Boilroaster?* he asked.

Dame Quickly and the Boilroaster

Yes, we said—Fred Seaman took us over to Locust Valley the other evening. (Suddenly a horrid thought struck us. We had thought that Fred had given us that lift over to Locust Valley just in the goodness of his heart. But now we wondered——)

When he left, he put in our hand a handsome book all about the *Boilroaster*. That, we felt, was the first step in breaking down our "sales resistance," as they say in the *Business e19 Course* up at Columbia.

We've been reading that book, and we want to say that the chaps who write that sort of literature are cunning fellows, and masters of a very insinuating prose style. They begin with a very pretty frontispiece of a *Boilroaster* car standing, all alone and dazzling-new, in a magnificent landscape of snow-clad peaks and clear lakes. How the *Boilroaster* got way up there (evidently somewhere near Banff) without any one driving her, and without even a speck of dust on her fenders, is a mystery. But there she is. Perhaps the man who drove her all those miles from the nearest distributing agency is at the bar of the C. P. R. Hotel, off behind those pine forests.

All the highbrow critics will tell you that the truly great writers are lovers of Beauty. Well, the anonymous author of the *Boilroaster* book is as keen a champion of Beauty as any one we ever heard of. And not only beauty, but refinement, too. There are two whole pages giving little pictures of "refinements." This is a book, we think, that could be put in the hands of the young without any hesitation. In fact, that is just where we did put it, for the urchin is cutting out the

[111]

The Powder of Sympathy

pictures of *Boilroasters* at this very minute. The whole
trend of Advertising nowadays (we wonder if they men-
tion this in the lectures on Advertising Psychology up
at Columbia) is to give delight to children. We would
hate to tell the Cunard Line and the International Mer-
cantile Marine Company how many of their folders our
juveniles have scissored up with shouts of delight.

The *Boilroaster* book is going to be a lesson to us.
We don't know if we will ever own a *Boilroaster*, but we
are certain that before we do we have got to spruce up
and be a bit more genteel. At present, we would be a
bit of anticlimax riding in a car like that. There is
"new beauty in its double bevel body line." We want
to look a bit more streamline ourself before we go in for
one. There are "massive head lamps, graceful cowl
lights, the louvres are more in number and their edges
show a smart touch of gold." There is "a courtesy
light illuminating the left side of the car," and a ventila-
tor in the cowl. We don't know exactly what the cowl
is, or the louvres, or at any rate we've never discovered
them in Dame Quickly.

Just as we are writing this, we see a headline in the
papers (in the *Evening Post*, to be accurate) about Sir
Charles Higham, who "Sees Advertising as a Great
Moral Force." We know of no writer who has a more
solid appreciation of moral forces than the author of
our *Boilroaster* brochure. What he has to say about
"sheer merit," "sound principles," "elimination of
waste," "combination of beauty and utility," "superi-
ority and refinement," "good taste" and "harmony of
colour" makes this work a genuine essay in æsthetics.

Dame Quickly and the Boilroaster

Moreover, we like his rational eclecticism. When the car has a 126-inch wheelbase, it makes it very easy riding and gives it charming "roadability." When it has a 119-inch wheelbase, it "gives a short turning radius which makes it remarkably easy to handle." Even in the least details, our author has an eye for loveliness. He confesses himself struck by "the attractive grouping of instruments on the dash, which emphasizes *Boilroaster* individuality." The upholstery, he says, is "restful." The folding seat for the extra passenger is "in reality a comfortable chair." And when we learn that the opalescent dome and corner lamps "provide enough light for reading," our only regret is that he doesn't add a suggested list of readings for tenants of a *Boilroaster* Enormous Eight.

Unhappily space is lacking to tell you in detail what a competent and winning fellow this author is. In the scientific portions of the work he rivals Fabre—in regard to the clutch, he says "the driven member is a single spider rotating between two rings." His passion for elegance, comfort, simplicity, and economy has never been surpassed—no, not by Plato or Walter Pater. The only drawback about his essay is that we feel we could never live up to the vehicle he describes.

VACATIONING WITH DE QUINCEY

I

HAVING severed our telephone wire and instructed the office boys to tell all callers that we are out at lunch, we look forward to a happy summer. We are going to begin enjoying ourself by systematically exploring the books in the library of the *Evening Post*. On a top shelf, well sprinkled with dust, we have found the excellent collected edition of De Quincey, in fourteen volumes, edited by David Masson. It is true that the first four volumes seem to have disappeared; but even if we begin at Volume V we calculate we shall find enough to keep us entertained for some time.

After we have finished De Quincey we are going to tackle P. T. Barnum's *Struggles and Triumphs*, a book that has long tempted us. We think kindly of the Founding Fathers of the *Post* for having assembled all these interesting volumes for our pleasure.

We have begun De Quincey with Volume V—*Biographies and Biographic Sketches*. Some of this—par-

Vacationing with De Quincey

ticularly the Joan of Arc—has a faintly familiar taste: perhaps we were made to read it at school. But we do not think we ever read before the magnificent essay on Charles Lamb. There is a long interpolated passage about Joan of Arc which does not seem to have anything to do with Lamb. Perhaps the *North British Review* (in which the essay first appeared in 1848) paid its contributors on a space basis. But, ejecting this parenthesis, it is certainly noble stuff. Moreover, it is interesting to note that at the time De Quincey wrote, Lamb was by no means established on the pinnacle of security as a permanent brightness in our literature. De Quincey writes as though consciously contradicting some opposition. It seems odd to hear him speak of people who "regard him [Lamb] with the old hostility and the old scorn."

We had intended not to introduce any quotations, for in this very volume De Quincey makes some stinging remarks about people who pad out their copy by interlarding material from stronger fists. But indeed the following passage seems to us so near the top of prose felicity that we lapse from grace:

In regard to wine, Lamb and myself had the same habit, viz., to take a great deal *during* dinner, none *after* it. Consequently, as Miss Lamb (who drank only water) retired almost with the dinner itself, nothing remained for men of our principles, the rigour of which we had illustrated by taking rather too much of old port before the cloth was drawn, except talking; amœbean colloquy, or, in Dr. Johnson's phrase, a dialogue of "brisk reciprocation." But this was impossible; over Lamb, at this period of his life, there passed regularly,

[115]

The Powder of Sympathy

after taking wine, a brief eclipse of sleep. It descended upon him as softly as a shadow. In a gross person, laden with superfluous flesh, and sleeping heavily, this would have been disagreeable; but in Lamb, thin even to meagreness, spare and wiry as an Arab of the desert or as Thomas Aquinas wasted by scholastic vigils, the affection of sleep seemed rather a network of aërial gossamer than of earthly cobweb—more like a golden haze falling upon him gently from the heavens than a cloud exhaling upwards from the flesh. Motionless in his chair as a bust, breathing so gently as scarcely to seem certainly alive, he presented the image of repose midway between life and death, like the repose of sculpture; and, to one who knew his history, a repose affectingly contrasting with the calamities and internal storms of his life.

De Quincey's essay on Lamb, like so many of the great critiques of the early nineteenth century, was originally written as a book review. We like to imagine what a *Blackwood* or *Edinburgh* reviewer would have said if the editor (in the manner of to-day) had told him to deal with a volume in 500 or 1,000 words. The nineteenth century reviewer took a spacious view of his job. Of this particular essay, which purported to be a notice of Talfourd's *Final Memorials of Charles Lamb* (1848), De Quincey said (very nobly):

Liberated from this casual office of throwing light upon a book, raised to its grander station of a solemn deposition to the moral capacities of man in conflict with calamity—viewed as a return made into the chanceries of heaven upon an issue directed from that court to try the amount of power lodged in a poor desolate pair of human creatures for facing the very anarchy of

[116]

Vacationing with De Quincey

storms—this obscure life of the two Lambs, brother and sister (for the two lives were one life), rises into grandeur that is not paralleled once in a generation.

Of course, De Quincey was a celestial kind of reviewer. Not even opium could make most of us write like that. Also he had the right idea about dealing with correspondence and accumulated papers. He used to live in one set of lodgings until the mass of miscellaneous matter filled the room. Then he would move to other quarters, leaving the pile in charge of the landlady. He always took care not to inform her of the new address.

There is a great deal more to be said about this Volume V, but we must skip along. (There is no reason, you know, why you shouldn't look up the book for yourself.) We will just be generous enough to pass on De Quincey's anecdote about how Coleridge first became a great reader. Coleridge, as a child, was going down the Strand in a day dream, imagining himself swimming the Hellespont. Moving his hands as though swimming, he happened to touch a gentleman's pocket. The latter thought him a young pickpocket. "What! so young and yet so wicked?" The boy, terrified, sobbed a denial, and explained that he had been imagining himself as Leander. The gentleman was so pleased that he gave him a subscription to a circulating library.

The next volume of De Quincey that we intend to study is X, in which we find *Letters to a Young Man Whose Education Has Been Neglected.* We are rather

The Powder of Sympathy

stricken to note that these were addressed to a young
man who was exactly the same age as ourself.

The first of these letters was evidently in the nature
of a Christmas present to the young gentleman, known
to us only as Mr. M. It is dated December 24, 1824.
Whether Mr. M. was an actual person and drew this
letter from his stocking on Christmas morning we are
not informed. Our own conjecture is that he was as
mythical as his sister-in-lore Miss M., of Walter de la
Mare's *Memoirs of a Midget*. Somehow there is a
humorous lack of reality in the way De Quincey intro-
duces him. Mr. M. is in possession of "great opulence,
unclouded reputation, and freedom from unhappy con-
nexions." Also he had "the priceless blessing of un-
fluctuating health." And yet he exhibited "a general
dejection." This, a young lady of seventeen told De
Quincey, "was well known to arise from an un-
fortunate attachment in early life." But finally De
Quincey exhumed the truth. Mr. M. had been de-
frauded of education. And Mr. M.'s first inquiry is
whether at his present age of 32 it would be worth his
while to go to college.

No, indeed, is De Quincey's unhesitant reply. Mr.
M. would be 12 or 14 years older than his fellow-stu-
dents, which would make their association "mutually
burthensome." And as for the value of college lec-
tures—

These whether public or private, are surely the very
worst modes of acquiring any sort of accurate knowl-
edge, and are just as much inferior to a good book on
the same subject as that book hastily read aloud, and

[118]

Vacationing with De Quincey

then immediately withdrawn, would be inferior to the
same book left in your possession, and open at any hour
to be consulted, retraced, collated, and in the fullest
sense studied.

It appears that the dejected young man, despite—
or perhaps on account of—his lack of education,
nourished a secret desire to be a writer. He had been
reading Coleridge's *Biographia Literaria*, particularly
the chapter called *An Affectionate Exhortation to Those
Who in Early Life Feel Themselves Disposed to Become
Authors*. According to De Quincey, Mr. M. asks his
opinion on Coleridge's views of this topic. Alas! now
we are more convinced than ever that Mr. M. is only a
phantom: unquestionably De Quincey, the canny
super-journalist, wafted him from the opium flagon as
an ingenious target for some anti-Coleridge banter.
His chaff directed at Coleridge is gorgeous enough. It
is double-decked chaff, too; for he not only affection-
ately twits his fellow opium-eater *in propria persona*,
but introduces for discussion an anonymous "eminent
living Englishman," who is plainly also Coleridge. He
compares C. with Leibnitz for his combination of fine
mind with a physique of equine robustness. This pas-
sage somehow causes us to chuckle aloud—

They were centaurs—heroic intellects with brutal
capacities of body. What partiality in nature! In
general, a man has reason to think himself well off in
the great lottery of this life if he draws the prize of a
healthy stomach without a mind; or the prize of a fine
intellect with a crazy stomach; but that any man should
draw both is truly astonishing.

[119]

The Powder of Sympathy

The first letter concludes with a charmingly humorous discussion of the problem (valid now as then) how a man of letters may get any creative work done and at the same time keep his wife and children happy.

II

Old Bill Barron, up in the composing room, asks us when we are going to take our Vacation. We are taking it now, we reply, reading De Quincey. Certainly we can't imagine why any one with as pleasing a job as ours should have any right to go off on holiday. There are so many people in this town who have to spend their time reading the new books: we are going to enjoy ourself by dipping into the old ones. With one exception. We have found, in the office of the *Literary Review*, and immediately made off with, *L'Extravagante Personnalité de Jacques Casanova*, by Joseph Le Gras (Paris: Bernard Grasset). We read the first sentence—

Emporté dans une berline confortable, dont les coffres sont abondamment pourvus de viandes, de pâtés et de vins; une femme sur les genoux, une autre parfois à ses côtés qui se frotte amoureusement à lui; vêtu de riches vêtements, le jabot et les manchettes enjolivés de fines dentelles, les goussets garnis de montres précieuses, le ventre chatouillé de breloques, les doigts étincelants de bagues, les poches tintant d'or et le mollet caressé dans la soie; réclamant à grand bruit les meilleurs chevaux aux relais, la plus belle chambre dans les auberges, jetant sa bourse à l'hôtelier et repartant au milieu des révérences et des courbettes; tel nous apparaît, en une attitude un peu conventionelle, l'aventurier Casanova au temps de sa splendeur.

Vacationing with De Quincey

That, of course, is one way of taking a Vacation.
We remember, with a small behind-the-arras chuckle,
one of Pearsall Smith's *Trivia* called "Lord Arden,"
which deliciously hits off the buried Casanova in all of
us. At any rate, we shall read this book about Extrav-
agant Jack.

But we must get back to De Quincey, or you'll think
we are purposely avoiding the topic. We hardly know
where to resume our prattle about this glorious creature.
Perhaps the first thing to note is an advisable shift in
viewpoint. Nowadays we are all introduced to De
Quincey at school, so his name comes to us with a
peculiar mixture of sublimity and painful awe—for
we learn that he was a wicked opium eater. We do not
realize that a number of his contemporaries regarded
him as a low-down dog of a journalist. Southey, for
instance, called him "one of the greatest scoundrels
living," and urged Hartley Coleridge to go to Edin-
burgh with a strong cudgel and give De Quincey a pub-
lic drubbing as "a base betrayer of the hospitable
social hearth." What was the cause of this peevish-
ness? Why, of course, the *Reminiscences of the
English Lake Poets*, a book whose social indiscretion
is exceeded only by its magnificently fecund humour;
told, like all De Quincey's waggishness, with a rich
sonorous volubility and luxurious plenitude of verbal
skill. There is a subtle wickedness of amusement in
the apparent solemnity of De Quincey's polysyllables.
The indignation caused latterly by such books as Mar-
got Asquith's was nothing compared to the anger of the
Lake Poets when they found their innocent privacies

The Powder of Sympathy

laid bare by the Opium Eater's pen. The Lakers took
themselves as seriously as groups of humanitarians al-
ways do. And they were quite right. Francis Thomp-
son complains that Milton never forgot he was Milton
—"but we must admit it was worth remembering."
Yet the domestic affairs of Wordsworth, Coleridge, and
Southey were indeed irresistibly comic. We have not
forgotten that Hartley Coleridge, whose childhood was
so charmingly enshrined in a poem by Wordsworth—

> Thou fairy voyager, that dost float
> In such clear water that thy boat
> May rather seem
> To brood on air than on an earthly stream—

also floated in liquids more ruddy. He was removed
from his fellowship at Oxford on the charge of drink-
ing too much—which must have been a very great deal
in the Oxford of those days.

Reminiscences of the Lake Poets is the kind of
book (Boswell's *Tour to the Hebrides* is another)
that causes indignation to the victims, but intense de-
light to posterity. Posterity always has the best of us,
anyhow. The anecdote of Coleridge's father and the
protruding shirt has always seemed to us one of the most
disgracefully amusing minutiæ in literature—and yet
even now, after a hundred years of sanctity, we are not
sure whether we ought to reprint it. Well, you can buy
Reminiscences of the Lake Poets in the Everyman
Series.

The next thing to be said about De Quincey is that
he would have been a glorious editor for one of Mr.

Vacationing with De Quincey

Hearst's newspapers. He wrote a good deal better than Mr. Arthur Brisbane; but he had the same acute instinct as to what the public is really interested in. We believe it was James L. Ford who described the Hearstian doctrine of newspaper policy as "Plenty of crime and plenty of underclothes." De Quincey was a glutton for crime. Did you know that he lost his job as editor of the *Westmoreland Gazette* because for sixteen months he filled its columns mainly with news of local lawbreaking? His employers did not appreciate genius. His instinct was absolutely sound. In spite of the disclaimers of refined people, crime news, when written not merely vulgarly but with earnestness and art, is one of the most valuable features of any journal. If we were running a newspaper we would begin by scouring the press clubs for a young De Quincey.

He had, we say, the newspaper man's instinct. Writing of the appalling Williams murders in 1811, he complains that though the outrage was committed shortly after midnight on Sunday morning, nothing reached the papers until Monday. "To have met the public demand for details on the Sunday, which might so easily have been done by cancelling a couple of dull columns and substituting a circumstantial narrative . . . would have made a small fortune. By proper handbills dispersed through all quarters of the infinite metropolis, 250,000 extra copies might have been sold."

This occurs in the postscript to *Murder as One of the Fine Arts*. In that immortal essay itself the macabre humour and the sledge-hammer impact of

The Powder of Sympathy

irony are probably a bit too grim and a bit (also) too learned and crushing for the gentler sort of reader. But the postscript, dated 1854, is the kind of horrific febrifuge that turns the heart to an Eskimo patty. We suggest that you try reading it aloud to a house party if you want to see blenching and shudders. The ultimate tribute to any writing of the narrative kind is to read it perpetually running ahead, in a horrid tension of eagerness, meanwhile holding one's proper "place" with a finger until one can force the eye back to pursue a methodical course. We ourself read that postscript thus, late at night in a lonely country house; and, by a noble summation of horror, Gissing began to growl and bristle as we reached the climax. We should hate to admit with what paltry quaverings we went forth into the night, where the trees were smoke-colour in a pallid moonglow, to see what was amiss. It was only a wandering dog prowling about. But for a few moments we had felt certain that our harmless Salamis Estates were thickly ambushed with assassins. It then required a trip to the icebox, and a considerable infare upon a very ammoniac Roquefort cheese, to restore tranquillity.

III

But we were talking about De Quincey. Yesterday was by no means a day wasted, for we got our amiable friend Franklin Abbott into our clutches, made him take a note of *Reminiscences of the English Lake Poets* (in the Everyman Series, we repeat) and insisted to him that for a man of genteel tastes this is one of the

Vacationing with De Quincey

most entertaining works ever printed. And also by
mere chance, which so often disposes the bright frag-
ments of life into a ruddy and high-spirited pattern, we
stopped in at a bookshop on Church Street just to say
howdy to the eccentric Raymond Halsey. Happening
to remark that it is now just a hundred years since
the *Confessions of an English Opium-Eater* was pub-
lished, Raymond disappeared with a rabbit-like scut-
tling motion; was heard digging among shelves at the
rear, and returned with the smile of one who thinks
he foresees a sale. It was a first edition of the *Opium
Eater* with the magical imprint of Taylor & Hessey.
Was there ever a more sacred name among publishers?
We don't need to remind you they were Keats's pub-
lishers, too. "Only fifty dollars," said Raymond,
but it was lunch time and we had to leave.

In the dark rear chamber of a Cedar Street tavern,
in that corner underneath the photographs of the
"Cheshire Cheese," something happened that seemed to
us almost as pretty as anything published by the vanish-
ed Taylor & Hessey. Frank spied an old friend of his,
a fellow Pittsburger, and the latter halted at our table
on his way out. We complimented him upon the fine
bronze patina of his countenance, to which he replied
that he had been salmon fishing. "You know," he said,
"there are only three salmon-flies that I care a con-
tinental for," and from his pocket he drew a small pink
envelope. With a tender hand he slid its contents onto
the board. "There they are," he said. His voice
seemed to change. "Dusty Miller, Durham Ranger,
and Jock Scott." The little feathery trinkets, glowing

The Powder of Sympathy

with dainty treacheries, lay there on the ale-bleached wood. Certainly it seemed to us there was poetry in that moment. "I go to Bingham, Maine," he said, "and drive eighteen miles up the Kennebec." (A small postern door opened gently upon another world.) "Old So-and-so is waiting at the station. He's always there. I could leave to-night; he'd be sure to be there when the train got in."

We had a perfectly vivid picture of old So-and-so waiting at the Bingham station. Yes, we could see him. Then the postern door closed, gently but definitely, with that strong pneumatic piston that is attached to all our doors.

We were saying, however, that De Quincey's *Reminiscences of the Lake Poets* caused great indignation among the Grasmere coterie. This was due not to any malice in De Quincey's manner of writing, which was affectionate and admiring throughout. It was due to something far more painful than malice—the calm, detailed, candid, and minute dissection of their lives. There was truly something astoundingly clinical in this microscopy. For instance, to take the case of Wordsworth's household, these are some of the comments De Quincey makes:

(1) That Mrs. Wordsworth—whose charm and simplicity he adores—was cross-eyed.

(2) That Dorothy—Wordsworth's sister—was a fervid and noble character, but stammered and was ungraceful.

(3) That Wordsworth's appearance grew less attractive with advancing age.

Vacationing with De Quincey

(4) That his legs were very ill-shapen and "were pointedly condemned by all female connoisseurs in legs." And that his shoulders were drooping and narrow.

(5) "The mouth, and the whole circumjacencies of the mouth, composed the strongest feature in Wordsworth's face." In fact, they reminded De Quincey of Milton.

(6) That he aged very rapidly—when thirty-nine he was taken to be over sixty.

(7) That his brother John, a sea captain, had lost his ship while drunk.

(8) That Wordsworth cannot have been amiable as a child.

(9) That the only time Wordsworth was drunk was as an undergraduate at Cambridge on visiting the rooms once occupied by Milton.

(10) That he had not the temperament ever to be an attractive wooer, and that it was "perplexing" that he had ever married.

(11) That he had had astonishing good luck in financial matters.

(12) That the Wordsworth menage was excessively plain and severe in simplicity.

(13) That Wordsworth and Southey did not really like each other.

(14) That Wordsworth treated books very barbarously, and used to cut the pages with a butter-smeared knife.

(15) That Wordsworth's library was meagre and insignificant compared to Southey's.

These are only a few of De Quincey's remarks, digested to their naked gist; by which they lose all the amusing complexity of comment wherein they are folded. But the précis will suffice to show that, whether consciously or not, they were exactly calculated

The Powder of Sympathy

to wound, with very deep incision, the most delicate
sensibilities of an austere, somewhat humourless and
extremely self-regarding man.

IV

On the 13th of February, 1848, De Quincey received
a letter asking him to contribute a writing of some sort
for an "album," to be sold at a Ladies' Bazaar. This
was to be held in March of that year, for the benefit of
the Library of the Glasgow Athenæum, and the ladies
begged him to reply by "return of post." This incident
in itself sounds contemporary enough to give us a fellow
feeling with De Quincey.

He had nothing available to send to the bazaar, but
there was one unfailing resource—his bathtub. Let
him describe it:

> In my study I have a bath, large enough to swim in,
> provided the swimmer, not being an ambitious man, is
> content with going ahead to the extent of three inches
> at the utmost. This bath, having been superseded
> (as regards its original purpose) by a better, has yielded
> a secondary service to me as a reservoir for my MSS.
> Filled to the brim it is by papers of all sorts and sizes.
> Every paper written *by* me, *to* me, *for* me, *of* or *concern-*
> *ing* me, and, finally, *against* me, is to be found, after an
> impossible search, in this capacious repertory. Those
> papers, by the way, that come under the last (or hostile)
> subdivision are chiefly composed by shoemakers and
> tailors—an affectionate class of men, who stick by one
> to the last like pitch-plasters.

De Quincey decided that the only thing to do was
to draw something at random from the bathtub for the

Vacationing with De Quincey

ladies' album. Accordingly, he made a little ceremony
of it. "Three young ladies, haters of everything un-
fair," were called in as referees; and a young man to do
the actual dipping. There were to be four dips into
the tub, and, for some reason not quite clear to us, the
young man was made to attire himself in a new potato-
sack, with holes cut for his legs and only his right arm
free. It would have been more to the purpose, we should
have thought, to blindfold him; but he was instructed
to dip at random, holding his face "at right angles to
the bath." He was to be allowed one minute to rum-
mage at random among "the billowy ocean of papers,"
and at the command *Haul Up!* was to come forth with
whatever his fingers approved. Before the ceremony
began a glass of wine was brought. De Quincey pro-
posed the health of the ladies of the Athenæum, and
pledged his honour that whatever MS. should be
dredged up would be sent off to the bazaar. And this,
he protested, though somewhere buried in the bath
there lay a paper which he valued as equal to the half
of his possessions.

But he was compelled to depart from the strict rigour
of his scheme. For let us see what the young man dis-
covered in the bathtub. The first dip brought up a
letter still unopened. It proved to be a dinner invita-
tion for the 15th of February. De Quincey was con-
gratulating himself on the success of his raffle, which
had thus enabled him to answer this letter without
irreparable breach of manners, when the young lady
referees discovered that the letter was four years old.

Number 2 was a "dun." The young man was, to De

The Powder of Sympathy

Quincey's dismay, dredging in a portion of the tub rich in overdue bills. "It is true," he says, "that I had myself long remarked that part of the channel to be dangerously infested with duns. In searching for literary or philosophic paper, it would often happen for an hour together that I brought up little else than variegated specimens of the dun." And so Number 3 was also a dun.

Number 4 turned out "a lecture addressed to myself by an ultra-moral friend—a lecture on procrastination, and not badly written." And this also De Quincey refused to allow to be sent to the Athenæum. So everything hinged on the fifth and extra dip, which was committed to one of the young ladies. She blushed rosily (De Quincey assures us) at the responsibility, and earnestly "ploitered" among the papers for full five minutes. "She contended that she knew, by intuition, the sort of paper on which duns were written: and, whatever else might come up, she was resolved it should not be a dun." "Don't be too sure," said De Quincey; but when the paper was finally drawn out it was a blank sheet.

This, the referees maintained, was a judgment on De Quincey, and meant that he should use the empty page to begin a new and original contribution for the ladies of Glasgow. Which he did, and turned out a little essay, suggested by their recent sport, on *Sortilege and Astrology*. We have tried to read it, but so far without success.

We are interested to note that others besides ourself have been turning back to De Quincey. In a recent

Vacationing with De Quincey

Fortnightly Review there is an article by H. M. Paull, sound enough in its observations, but grievously lacking in style. Mr. Paull, moreover, seems to us to shoot too far when he says that "to modern readers De Quincey's efforts to be sprightly only cause annoyance." It is true that sometimes his astonishing verbosity and his passion for footnotes outrun a hasty temper; but for our part we find something notably odd and agreeable in his queer, preposterous humour. His habit of calling great men familiarly by their first names—Dr. Johnson is "Sam," and even the learned and ancient Josephus becomes "Joe," and Thomas à Kempis "Tom"—is deplored by Mr. Paull; but this habit, we fear, has been inherited by columnists, and we had better not defend it too vigorously. The bathtub anecdote, which we have pared down until it loses most of its gusto, is, in the original, not devoid of humour. (Volume XIII of the collected works.)

And De Quincey's ramified and rambling way of narrative offers surprising delights in unexpected parentheses. For instance, in the *Opium Eater* he happens to mention a murder that had been committed on Hounslow Heath. "The name of the murdered person was Steele, and he was the owner of a lavender plantation in that neighbourhood." A lavender plantation! There is a fragrant circumstance for the mind of a poet to dwell on. Think of the chance immortality of the unlucky Steele—deathless now, because (poor devil) he was murdered and had a lavender plantation.

THE SPANISH SULTRY

TURNING up masterpieces of unintentional humour is a pleasant diversion of most writers. Everyone has his own favourites—on this side Atlantic many students vouch for *The Balsam Groves of Grandfather Mountain* (by Shepherd M. Dugger) as the most amusing book written in America; in Britain a few diligent explorers beat the drum for *Irene Iddesleigh*, a novel written by Mrs. Amanda McKittrick Ros (of Belfast). Neither of these books, unhappily, is easy to lay hand upon. But as a possible competitor, how do you like *The Spanish Sultry*, by Ambrose Dargason (Harrisburg, 1905)? We have no copy, but once we took down some extracts.

Mr. Dargason's hero was a window-glass merchant "whose nature was as transparent and reflective as the goods he throve in." This merchant's name was Wilbert Vocks; after his retirement from merchandise he

The Spanish Sultry

spent his time in travelling about looking for a suitable wife to inherit his fortune. Unhappily, his inherent caution always caused him to sheer off just when the reader was expecting the happy nuptials. The scene on the park bench in Harrisburg, one moony evening, is a favourite of ours:

In the anæmic brightness of the crescendo moon Frederica's eyes were gilded with the splendor of her sex's softest charms. They were frosted bulbs of allure, and Wilbert trenched delicately upon her French-shod toes as a symbol of hardy waxing tenderness.

"Oh, Mr. Vocks," said she, the beautiful coamings of her orbs brimming over with cheer, "how many equinoxes will hereafter wax and wane, search through this garden, but for one in vain."

"You are quoting the Rubaiyat," said he, "but with indifferent adhesion to the text."

"Adhesion," she replied, "was never one of my frailties," and a trifle peaked [sic] withdrew to the distant angle of the iron settee.

Wilbert's momentary harshness had already dissipated and he regretted this intrusion of pedantic nicety upon the moonlit promise of their double entente. "I bespeak a rapproachment," he gallantly murmured and, sliding deftly along the parallel rods of metal subforming the trysting bench, found himself chilled by coming en rapport with a section of the seat not warmed by humane contact.

"But you must not reproach me," she taunted shyly. "It is too plain that you were not brought up in Harrisburg, where men speak chivalrously to women and good breeding is a native filament of the tender air."

"Probably you are cold on that hitherto unfrequented segment of iron slatting," he said, shrivelling his inward tremolo by an affection of stern brusque. "Why not

The Powder of Sympathy

slide over this way a little, and chivalry commends my sheltering you from the sharp fidgetings of frost which, however commendable to coal dealers, betray the softer passions to gooseflesh and eventual snivel."

Womanly, without further quibble, she responded, and the beauty of that unsophisticated face was shielded soon from external examination by the protective polygon of his arm and elbow. It was a generous moment, and in harmony with all the higher laws of human sentiment.

The delighted reader might be pardoned for thinking that in this idyllic scene the restless affections of Mr. Vocks had found satisfaction. But Frederica, after several evenings of intellectual interchange, proved too shallow for his deep-laden mind. As Mr. Dargason put it (his taste for oddly mixed nautical metaphors was rather extreme):

He grounded upon the shoals of her mentality and, after striving vainly to warp off into deeper areas of thought and sentiment, was forced to broach his cargo of affection upon the outgoing tides. Only thus, by careening and jettisoning his rich hatches of emotional freight, and scudding forth under bare poles and jury rigging, was he able to win clear to the open sea of freedom, escaping the lee shores of an uncongenial union. The bright occulting lamps of her eyes shone like desperate beacons, but he remembered that lighthouses are intended not to allure the cautious mariner, but to warn him away. He reefed his binnacle gravely, and with only an aching heart throbbing in the empty hatches of his personality determined henceforward to steer by the unquestionable stars of intuition. Her soundings were too easily fathomed. In a word, she was not deep enough.

The Spanish Sultry

To quiet his melancholy, Mr. Vocks returns into the busy world of trade. We have not space for very full quotation, but his discussion with his business associates is worth a brief extract:

As surely as my name is Wilbert Vocks (he said), I intend that this business shall be conducted in accord with all principles of integrity and without demurrage to trickery. I have been allowed by fortune to make a frugal and circumstantial inspection of the general laws and accidents of life, and it is my conviction that by exploring the estuaries of remorse no bill of lading was ever brought to consummation. My rudder is uncompromisingly turned to the favoring gales of expedience, and we will sail a vigorous course into the latitudes of magnetism.

In this admirable resolution Mr. Vocks was strengthened by his partner (Mr. Henry Shingle), who is described as "a thrifty man the colour of a glass of light beer, bleached brown by an open-air youth in Monongahela County, but surmounted spiritually by the bright bubbles of aspiration and elasticity. His clothes were neat and his habits orderly; of his meditative components it is not necessary to surmise. He had not made a habit of thinking profoundly, for he knew that any thought he might have could easily be rebutted by more carefully trained men; therefore he spared himself the embarrassment of argument. His management of the Sales Department, however, was not to be criticized."

We wish we had taken the trouble to copy out more of *The Spanish Sultry* while we were about it. The Sultry herself was the lady to whom Mr. Vocks finally

The Powder of Sympathy

succumbed: she caused the fracture of the window-glass business. As the author put it: "Hers was not the clear transparence of Mr. Vocks's glassy nature; she was stained with violent and ominous colours, and through the panes of her vehement character there burst downpours of scarlet and lavender trouble."

WHAT KIND OF A DOG?

WHAT kind of a dog is he?" said the Sea Cliff vet-
erinary over the phone.

We must confess we were stumped. All we could
say was that he is—Oh, well just a kind of a dog. We
didn't like to say that he is a Synthetic Hound, and
that his full name is Haphazard Gissing I. We didn't
like to admit, at any rate over the telephone, that one
of his grandmothers may have been a dachshund and
that certainly one of his brothers-in-law is an Airedale.
But at any rate it was fixed that we should take our
excellent Gissing over to the kennels to be boarded
while we were in the city.

Gissing's behaviour was odd. He seemed, in some
inscrutable way, to suspect that something was going
to happen. The night before his departure he disap-
peared, and was away all night—saying good-by to his

The Powder of Sympathy

cronies, we suppose. When we came home early in the afternoon to convoy him to Sea Cliff he was nowhere to be found. But about suppertime he turned up, looking more haggard and disreputable than ever. There was a fresh scar on his face, and he was very hungry. He ate his supper hurriedly, with no dignity at all. As soon as he heard the rattle of his chain his spirits went very low.

But the admirable creature was docile. Dogs are profoundly religious at heart: they put their trust in their deities. Unlike cats, who are determined atheists and fight to the last against fate, dogs accept calmly what they see is ordered by the gods. Gissing hopped into Dame Quickly without protest and sat in silence during the ride. His nose was unusually cold, but then that may have been only the winter evening. He had somewhat the bearing of one who is going to the dentist.

Dog fanciers are always baffled and set at naught when they see Gissing. But the Sea Cliff veterinarian made the most penetrating remark when we arrived. He is accustomed, indeed, to dogs of high degree—such dogs as are favoured by the North Shore of Long Island, and Gissing was rather a shock to him. After a long look, "What is his name?" he said. "Gissing," we replied, with just a little of that embarrassment we always feel when such questions are asked; for it is generally shown in the manner of the inquirer that Gissing is an unusual name, particularly for a dog who looks as though he ought to be called Rover. So we said, perhaps a little defiantly, "Gissing." But the Doctor misunderstood it. "Guessing!" he said du-

What Kind of a Dog?

biously, and looked again at the abashed quadruped. "That's because he keeps you guessing what breed he is."

It amuses us the more to have Gissing staying there, associating with the lordly dogs of Long Islanders who are spending the snow season in Florida, because we feel that it is rather like sending a child to a fashionable boarding school. It is probably useless as far as education is concerned, but it ought to be an interesting experience, and he may pick up a little polish. Gissing may make friends with some influential dogs who will be of help to him in future life; who knows? It is expensive, we admit; but since we paid nothing for him in the first place, and have used him liberally for copy, we feel that we owe Gissing this opportunity to improve himself. At any rate, he has promised to write us a letter from time to time, and we shall see how he gets on.

A LETTER FROM GISSING

DEAR FRIEND, I thought that as to-morrow is Valentine's Day I had better send you a line to report progress and to wish you my respectful greeting. This Dr. R with whom I am living is a fine man and he smells good to me I heard him say something about a Dog Show being on in New York now and I thought I ought to tell you what the old veterans in this veterinary hotel say, they say not to go to any such show because those things there are not Regular Dogs, not Red Blooded He Dogs not Dogs as you might say with the Bark On. Of course at first it was a bit hard for me here being as I am a self-made dog so to say and not accustomed to associate with pedigree folks and I rather wish you would send me a new collar, that old strap is about wore out and to tell you the truth there is a little Airedale flapper in the next cage that I would like to make an impression on, some of the boys have those collars that are studded with brass spikes and look mighty fine don't forget my size is 16. As I was

[140]

A Letter from Gissing

saying, at first things were a bit unpleasant, there is a big collie who looked me over the first morning I was here and said "Ye men, how do they get that way? Who let this mutt in here among cultivated animals?" Well, I wasn't going to stand for that stuff, so I talked right back to him and asked him if he had ever been in print, but I didn't get it across very big because he was so ignorant he didn't seem to realize what it means to have been written up right along in the *Evening Post*. By the way, I get kennel-sick for the old paper, out here they all read the sensational sheets and I wish you would tell the Circulation Manager to put me down for a two-months' subscription. All the other fellows here gave me the razz when I told them my name, Gissing, what kind of a name is that for a dog they said? I told them I was named after a Writer but none of the rough-necks ever heard of him. But I noticed right away that the little Airedale kid was interested, she seems to have some imagination her name is Mistress Zephine IV and I understand that the Airedales are a very fine family. I told her that it had been suggested by some that I had some Airedale in me too, and she laughed and looked a bit scandalized. Either you are an Airedale or you aren't, she said; there's no half and half measures. Live and learn, I told her. Anyway she and I go out for a walk together with one of the men every morning, and I have got her quite interested in books, she has promised to write me when she gets home and tell what kind of books her master reads. When you write, send me a cake of flea soap, I want to make my-

The Powder of Sympathy

self solid with this dame. There is a whole lot I could write about, but this is just to say that You are my Valentine. These dogs here all have three-barrelled names so I will sign myself in full,

Your affectionate dog,
HAPHAZARD GISSING I.

P. S. Please write right away and tell me what is the name of your publisher, I want to give one of your books to Zephine, when I told her you were a Writer she wouldn't believe it, I am talking you up big all the time here, but it is hard work to get away with it because appearances are against us; never mind, some day we will knock them cold; and what is the name of your car, one of these fellows here says he rides around in a Rolls Royce and I told him yours was a Dame Quickly and he says there isn't any such boat, it's an imported car I told him. Yes, he says, imported from Detroit; never mind, I've got them all guessing, they're all keen to see what kind of a guy you are, I told them the story about the old trousers, I guess it was a mistake.

H. G. I.

JULY 8, 1822

IT IS to-day a hundred years since that sultry after-
noon when Edward John Trelawny, aboard Byron's
schooner-yacht *Bolivar*, fretted anxiously in Leghorn
Harbour and watched the threatening sky.   The thun-
derstorm that broke about half-past six lasted only
twenty minutes, but it was long enough to drown both
Shelley and his friend Williams, very haphazard yachts-
men, who had set off a few hours earlier in their small
craft.   It was only some foolish red tape about quar-
antine that had prevented Trelawny from convoying
them in the *Bolivar;* in which case, probably, that
dauntless and all-competent adventurer could have
saved them.   He was already dubious of their navigat-
ing skill.   So, if there is any comfort in the thought, one
may conclude that Shelley—though of course doomed
to some tragic end, for skylarks do not die in nests—
was partly the victim of that invincible social and

bureaucratic stupidity against which he had always nobly chafed.

Those of our clients who care to devote this week-end to some meditation on Shelley and what he still means to us can well begin with Professor Firkins's excellent essay. Mr. Firkins, with his usual clarity, lays pen upon a number of considerations that have always occurred to Shelley's readers, but are not often carefully thought out. For our own part, we also have a mind to reread Francis Thompson's essay, which remains in our memory as a prismatic dazzle of metaphor. But there are two items which, if our high-spirited clients have not read, they should certainly take steps to meditate. Hogg's description of Shelley at Oxford is as lovely a picture of youthful genius as one is likely to find: and Trelawny's *Recollections of the Last Days of Shelley and Byron* gives the other panel of the portrait. It is surely not often that chance bequeaths us such sympathetic observers for both beginning and end of a great life. And then, of course, it is not impossible for our clients to recruit their imaginations by reading some of Shelley himself. If your hearts are what we like to think they are, you may

> Rise like Lions after slumber
> In unvanquishable number.

But, for information about Shelley, Trelawny is the darling of all hearts. There is something indescribably manly in his rough, cheery, potent narrative, with its amazing vigour and humour. "As a general rule," says

July 8, 1822

he, "it is wise to avoid writers whose works amuse or delight you, for when you see them they will delight you no more." But Shelley, he adds, was a grand exception to this very wise rule. One could happily spread several pages with excerpts from his good-humoured, observant companionship with Shelley and Byron. But, to commemorate the date now here, we intend to copy out part of his description of the burning of Shelley's body on the Italian coast. Fine and gruesome as it is, we cannot help believing it not well enough known among those younger clients whom we daily cudgel towards virtue. Trelawny says:

The lonely and grand scenery that surrounded us so exactly harmonized with Shelley's genius that I could imagine his spirit soaring over us. The sea was before us . . . not a human dwelling was in sight. As I thought of the delight Shelley felt in such scenes of loneliness and grandeur whilst living, I felt we were no better than a herd of wolves or a pack of wild dogs, in tearing out his battered and naked body from the pure yellow sand that lay so lightly over it, to drag him back to the light of day; but the dead have no voice, nor had I power to check the sacrilege. . . . Even Byron was silent and thoughtful. We were startled and drawn together by a dull hollow sound that followed the blow of a mattock; the iron had struck a skull, and the body was soon uncovered. Lime had been strewn upon it; this, or decomposition, had the effect of staining it of a dark and ghastly indigo color. Byron asked me to preserve the skull for him; but remembering that he had formerly used one as a drinking-cup, I was determined Shelley's should not be so profaned. The limbs did not separate from the trunk, as in the case of

The Powder of Sympathy

Williams's body, so that the corpse was removed entire into the furnace. I had taken the precaution of having more and larger pieces of timber, in consequence of my experience of the day before of the difficulty of consuming a corpse in the open air with our apparatus. After the fire was well kindled we repeated the ceremony of the previous day; and more wine was poured over Shelley's dead body than he had consumed during his life. This with the oil and salt made the yellow flames glisten and quiver. The heat from the sun and fire was so intense that the atmosphere was tremulous and wavy. The corpse fell open and the heart was laid bare. The frontal bone of the skull, where it had been struck with the mattock, fell off; and, as the back of the head rested on the red-hot bottom bars of the furnace, the brains literally seethed, bubbled, and boiled as in a cauldron, for a very long time.

Byron could not face this scene; he withdrew to the beach and swam off to the *Bolivar*. Leigh Hunt remained in the carriage. The fire was so fierce as to produce a white heat on the iron, and to reduce its contents to grey ashes. The only portions that were not consumed were some fragments of bones, the jaw, and the skull, but what surprised us all, was that the heart remained entire. In snatching this relic from the fiery furnace, my hand was severely burnt; and had any one seen me do the act I should have been put into quarantine.

After cooling the iron machine in the sea, I collected the human ashes and placed them in a box, which I took on board the *Bolivar*.

There are those still living who have shaken the hard, quick hand that snatched Shelley's heart from the coals. Sir Sidney Colvin, for instance, who tells much about Trelawny in his *Memories and Notes of Persons*

July 8, 1822

and Places. And ghastly as the above account may
seem to those of tender sensibility, the parable it im-
plies is too rich to be omitted. Lo! were they not words
of Shelley's that winged the greatest popular success
in recent fiction?* And, though lulled long ago by the
blue Mediterranean—

> The blue Mediterranean, where he lay,
> Lulled by the coil of his crystalline streams—

that burning, reckless heart survives to us little cor-
rupted by time—survives as a symbol of poetic energy
superior to the common routines of life. "Mighty
meat for little guests, when the heart of Shelley was laid
in the cemetery of Caius Cestius!"

---

*If Winter Comes.

MIDSUMMER IN SALAMIS

IN MIDSUMMER the morning walk to the station is
one long snuff of green and gold. On the winding
stony lane through the Estates, before you reach the
straight highway to the railroad, it is a continual sharp
intake through the nostrils, an attempt to savour and
identify the rich, moist smells of early day. That tangle
of woodland we would like to call by the good old English
word *spinney*, if only to haul in an equally ancient pun.
It is in the spinney that you get the top of the morning.
Dew is on the darkening blackberries. Little gauzy
cobwebs are spread everywhere on grass and bushes,
suggesting handkerchiefs dropped by revelling midnight
dryads. The little handkerchiefs are all very soppy—

Midsummer in Salamis

do the dryads suffer from hay fever? As you emerge
onto the straight station road, it is comforting if you
see, not far away, some commuter whose time-sense is
reliable trudging not too far ahead. When that long
perspective is empty anxiety fills the breast. Across
the level Long Island plain come occasional musical
whistles from trains on the other line—the Westbury
branch. But the practiced commuter knows his own
whistle and alarms not at alien shrillings.

In midsummer the subaltern life around us is grown
lusty. The spider is in his heyday and cannot be
denied. Even indoors he shrewdly penetrates. Look-
ing for a book along the shelves, our eye was caught by
the hasty climb of one small spinner, who had been
hanging on his airy cord apparently also scanning the
titles. To the top of the case he retired, beyond reach.
We wish him luck and hope no domestic besom may
find him. The young lumpish robins that used to
flutter heavily across the road, easily within grasp,
fat paunches of feathers upon incapable wings—these
are now strong of flight and cat-safe. The young
rabbits with whom our woods are crowded no longer
stand curiously in the roadway almost until our foot
is on them. They too are maturing and have learned
wise suspicion. The mole nightly increases his mean-
dering subway, which looks like a zigzagging varicose
vein on the surface of the lawn. And Gissing, untaught
by menace or thrashing, every night buffets down more
of the phlox plants so carefully set out by Titania, in
his caperings with a roving Airedale from no one knows
where. Only the pond noises seem to have lessened in

The Powder of Sympathy

vitality. The frogs are growing cynical, perhaps. In the sylvester midnight—thanks to Mr. C. E. Montague for that pretty phrase—they utter only an occasional disillusioned twangle, like the pluck of a loose bass string.

But there are signs that the Salamis Estates, so long a rustic Nirvana, are going to fall under the hand of civilization. Which will, one doubts not, have its advantages. It will be helpful to have gas to cook with; and sidewalks are enjoyable for baby carriages and velocipedes. But we shall never forget the happy Salamis Estates as they still are—the lonely roads through virgin woods; the little hidden lakes; the old abandoned orchard buried in overgrowth of vines and forest; solitude and sanctuary. It is our darling old horror of a Salamis railway station that has spared us the evils of "development." The casual passenger looking out on that gruesome pagoda of claret-coloured brick and the huddle of wooden shacks around it, can only think of Salamis as a place damned and forgotten. When some of our neighbours grunt about that station we think inwardly of it with affection. It has spared us much. There are some people, of course, who really like to live in an artificed toy park like Nassau Boulevard or Garden City. We were raised on the books of Mayne Reid and Du Chaillu; we are for the jungle.

Yet we would not admit impediments to progress, if it does not rob our rustic Eden of all its wilderness charm. And anyhow progress is coming willynil. Actually, in the past six months, we have seen several houses built on the outskirts of our region. The new

Midsummer in Salamis

Methodist kirk, though apparently halted temporarily while our good dominy raises some more funds, is already shoulder-high. Another church, years ago foundered to the status of a saloon, now does brisking business as garage. The little empty lodge at the entrance to the Estates, where we vote on election days, will some day be a tea-room, we suspect. It is ideal for that purpose, with its big open fireplace. In fact, we have heard influential Salamites say that it could be had almost rent-free by some really refined lady as a pekoe-saloon. Those who move the destinies of the Estates think that a nice tea-room there would help the tone of the neighbourhood. We pass this information on to ambitious ladies, on condition we are allowed to have three lumps and an extra pat of butter.

It is all very interesting, because we are going to have a unique opportunity to see exactly how civilization works. We have watched new signboards go up at the front and back entrances to the Estates. Not long ago a hundred thousand people might have gone by and never known our little world was there. We study the new board of a Mortgage Company announcing Desirable Plots. Yes, we can see a plot. Civilization is plotting to take us under its wing. We are going to have a good look at this thing they call civilization and see how it goes about it. Five years from now will we be able to see cows being driven home from their daily pasture near our Green Escape? We are not blind to omens. Just as lightning glimmers even through eyelids closed in bed, so behind the leafy screen of our still scatheless sanctum we can see the bright

The Powder of Sympathy

eyes of Real Estate men blazing in the sky. Well
. . . there are compensations. Our title is clean
and clear, and our second mortgage sticks to us closer
than a shinplaster. Wait till they try to buy us out;
we'll get some of our own back.

So we meditate, partly as poet and partly as Man
of Affairs, as we walk homeward up the hill. The
singing peanut-wagon of George Vlachos, steaming its
thin, pensive tune, comes clopping wearily down the
road, the white horse shambling a bit after a long day
on the highways. FRESH ROSTED PEANUTS, CANDY,
ICE CREAM, says the legend. We note the pile of fresh
shingles beside the little house going up near the sta-
tion; we sniff the tang of mortar where our good friend
Mr. Corliss will next year be preaching the word of
God in his new steeple-house (as George Fox would
have called it). We wonder where the Salamis Heights
movie will be, when it comes? That, and an occasional
street-lamp up in our tangled knolls, will make it easier
to keep servants, very likely. And think of having gas
to cook with instead of those oil stoves. . . . Yes,
perhaps civilization will have merits.

THE STORY OF GINGER CUBES

I

[A letter from the Proprietor of the Ginger Cubes to his Advertising Manager, who is ill in hospital.]

DEAR RUSSELL: When I heard that you had been taken to the hospital with a badly dislocated sense of proportion and exhaustion of the adjective secretions, I was worried. The doctor said that you were suffering from a severe attack of deprecation and under-statement, and I feared that would mean you would be quite unfit to help me in the forthcoming campaign for Ginger Cubes. But I hear now that a few weeks of silence and relaxation will bring you round. I have ordered the *Police Gazette* and *The Nation* to be sent you. Each in its own way is highly entertaining.

In our last conference, just before you were taken ill, you tried with your usual energy and bullheaded

The Powder of Sympathy

vitality to persuade me to say a word about the Ginger Cubes at the Paperhangers Convention. You made a great deal of the point that this would be a vast gathering, and that it would be excellent business for me to give them a "message."

I ask you to meditate this thought: give me a small group of folks who are more or less interested in the same sort of thing that I am, and I will "talk my head off." But speaking to large, miscellaneous audiences, many of whom are only incubating there to pass away the time until the theatres open, is my idea of loss of compression.

We have appropriated a fine promotion budget for the Ginger Cubes, but I am holding up any action until I can argue the situation with you. About newspaper advertising, for instance—I want your opinion as to the papers which are read (1) most carefully, (2) by the class of people to whom the Ginger Cubes are likely to appeal, (3) at the time of day when their minds (and palates) are receptive—i. e., morning or evening? For instance, do you think that people will be likely to be tempted by the Cubes in the morning, just after breakfast? I think not. I believe that the evening, in that faintness and debility that are supposed to attack office-workers on their way home (especially in the subway) is the psychological zero hour for the Ginger Cubes.

Miss Balboa, to whom I am dictating this, says that she never noticed any sign of weakness or lack of energy in the evening rush on the subway. I believe it is worth while to get the feminine reaction on this matter before we make any decisions. One thing I have always re-

The Story of Ginger Cubes

gretted about you as an Advertising Manager is that you are not married. Wives are often very helpful in these questions of merchandising strategy. But perhaps you can question some of the nurses at the hospital and get their reaction.

In regard to these mediums, the question of circulation does not cut any ice in my cynical and querulous mind. It is not a matter of circulation, but of penetration, that excites me.

The chemical laboratory reports that the Cubes will positively have a soothing and tonic effect upon the digestive organs, and that we are justified in saying so. Unfortunately they say that the Cubes cannot possibly be of any value in combating "pyorrhea," so we cannot go riding on the other folks' toothpaste copy. For your amusement, I have thought up this slogan:

> WHY NOT INVEST IN
> A NEW INTESTINE?
> TRY GINGER CUBES

Which is probably too startling. But anyhow, when we have decided, I wish our copy to be Cumulative, Concise, and Continuous. Then, ho for the Ginger Cubes!

Yours,

NICHOLAS RIBSTONE,

President The Ginger Cubes Corporation.

N.R./D.B.

The Powder of Sympathy

[A letter from the Proprietor of the Ginger Cubes to his Advertising Manager, who is ill in hospital.]

DEAR RUSSELL: I am glad to hear from Dr. Nichevo that you are doing well. He reports that in your delirium you had visions of nothing but full page insertions, so I realize that you must have been a very sick man. I am glad you are coming out of it. The Doctor says that a little quiet meditation on business problems will help to bring you back to "normalcy."

So you might think this over. I have just been telling the boys at our conference this morning that I want our advertising matter for the Ginger Cubes to be distinguished. I've been much impressed, for instance, by those ads that Childs restaurants have been running for some time, in which they make use of historians, philosophers, poets, and what not, to introduce the topic of food. I am wondering whether, in your extensive reading, you have come across any literature in which Ginger or Cubes have been written about in a pleasing, sentimental strain? Miss Balboa thinks that Shakespeare said something about Ginger being "hot in the mouth," but I am a little afraid of that word hot. How about

> THESE CUBES FROM THE SOUTH
> ARE WARM IN THE MOUTH

The Story of Ginger Cubes

What I want you to do is tell me what the resources
of literature are in the way of quotations about Ginger.

Some of the boys are much taken by a suggestion
that has come in from the Gray Matter Advertising
Agency, who somehow got wind of our plans. Mr.
Gray, the Psychology Director of Gray Matter Agency,
wants us to mark the cubes with little spots of white
sugar, so that they look like dice. Here's the joker:
he wants us to pack them in little boxes in which
half the cubes will be marked as five-spots and half
as deuces, using the slogan, They Always Turn Up
Seven.

That seems to me a bit complicated, but I must admit
that I'm rather struck by the idea of advertising the
Cubes as Digestive Dice. I'm having the idea of mark-
ing them with sugar spots looked into, to see what it
will cost. I visualize a subway poster showing the
cubes tumbling out of a dice shaker, with the words
Throw These for Good Health. Do you think that
is too distinctly masculine an appeal? But think of
getting this idea across to the lunching public, of always
carrying a box of the Ginger Cubes in their vest pocket
(we could have the box shaped like a little dice-shaker,
hey?), they can use them to throw for who is to pay the
check, and then eat them. Can you put that thought
in twelve words?

What a pity that neither of us is married, and has no
wife to fall back on for advice in this delicate matter.
Miss Balboa, my new stenographer, thinks that women
would not be attracted by this gambling note; she says
that women are born Dutch-treaters, and do not fall

The Powder of Sympathy

for the idea of settling the lunch-check by mere chance. Please see what the hospital nurses think about this.

This man Gray, from the Gray Matter Agency, is a whirlwind. He has shot in some suggestive layouts for car-cards that make my head spin. These are some of his aspirations—

```
          DIGESTIVE DICE
     MEAN LUCK FOR THE LIVER
        TRY  GINGER  CUBES
```

```
     FOR A CHEW IN THE TUBES
      CHOOSE GINGER CUBES
```

And he has doped out a map showing the whole digestive apparatus laid out like a subway system, and the Ginger Cubes keep traffic moving.

All this seems to me a bit too unconventional, although I confess I am amused by the originality. Tell me what your reaction is. I'm sending you some of the Cubes to distribute among the nurses.

Yours,

NICHOLAS RIBSTONE,

President The Ginger Cubes Corporation.

N.R./D.B.

The Story of Ginger Cubes

III

[A letter from Miss Candida Cumnor, one of the nurses at the Hippocrates Hospital, to Mr. Nicholas Ribstone, President of the Ginger Cubes Corporation.]

DEAR MR. RIBSTONE: Poor Mr. Russell is still very weak, and has not been able to write to you himself. Dr. Nichevo says that he has never seen a more interesting case of complete exhaustion of the salesmanship glands. He thinks that the patient must have been under a very severe strain for a long time preceding the breakdown. I gathered from what Mr. Russell said in his period of delirium that he had been trying to sell by mail order a complete set of Tolstoy's works, but by some mistake had bought the wrong mailing list from one of the houses that deal in such things. They gave him a list of members of the Ku Klux Klan, and the returns on his effort were so disheartening that it broke him all up. He was very queer for a while. But one delusion helped a great deal. He had a fixed idea that the temperature chart at the end of his bed was a sales graph, and the more peaks there were in it the better he was pleased, for he thought that at last the K. K. K. were beginning to fall for Tolstoy.

At any rate, he is much better now, and asks me to write to you for him. I must say that I think you picked a fine Advertising Manager for your Ginger Cubes: I have never seen such an enthusiastic fellow. The specimen drawings for car cards that you sent him are pinned up on a screen beside the bed, and he hardly

[159]

The Powder of Sympathy

takes his eyes off them. He has had all the nurses in the ward munching the Ginger Cubes, or Digestive Dice as he likes to call them, and is asking me to make a note of their opinions. He says he plans an interesting lay-out under the caption

COMMENTS OF THE MEDICAL PROFESSION
ON THE GINGER CUBES

I must admit that I find the Cubes very tasty and refreshing.

To show you that he is really picking up, I will tell you that this morning he asked me to send out to the nearest newsstand for a number of magazines and papers, which he has been looking through with close attention.

But I must not deceive you. In spite of his enthusiasm he is still very weak, and it will take a lot of building up before his merchandising centres are up to par. It would do no harm if you were to send him some stimulating books to read, such as Orison Swett Marden or Dr. Crane.

By the way, Mr. Ribstone, someone in your office has made a mistake in addressing letters to this hospital, the name of which is not Hypocrites but Hippocrates; the spelling is nearly the same but the pronunciation is different, after the name of a famous doctor of old times. Now I must draw to an end, for the patient needs attention; this is a long letter but he wanted you to know all about him.

Yours sincerely,
CANDIDA CUMNOR.

The Story of Ginger Cubes

IV

[A telegram from the National Drug Novelties Company to Nicholas Ribstone.]

Chicago, April 11, 1922.

Hear interesting rumour about new lozenge Ginger Cubes to be marketed by you would you consider entrance of outside capital in this venture or sell outright trade name formula and goodwill Believe you have a winner.

EDWARD GARTENBAUM,
President National Drug Novelties.

V

[A telegram from Nicholas Ribstone, president of the Ginger Cubes Corporation, to Edward Gartenbaum of the National Drug Novelties Company.]

Decline discuss selling interest in Ginger Cubes distribution plans perfected watch our smoke.

RIBSTONE.

VI

[A memorandum sent to heads of departments of the National Drug Novelties Company, Chicago.]

OFFICE BULLETIN No. 38946 (Series B).

Minutes of Conference Held in Directors' Room,
April 12.

Mr. Gartenbaum reported that he had had a telegram from Ribstone declining assistance in financing

The Powder of Sympathy

the Ginger Cubes. Mr. Gartenbaum thought the matter important enough to warrant calling the directors together. Was it possible that Ribstone had access to new sources of capital hitherto unemployed in the drug trade? This seemed unlikely in view of their own recent canvass. Mr. G. asked Mr. O'Keefe, who had just come back from New York, whether he had been able to find out anything definite about the plans for Ginger Cubes.

Mr. O'Keefe said that he had found the trade greatly interested in the rumours that had been current. It was said everywhere that Ribstone had got hold of a formula that was a knockout, and that the Ginger Cubes had caused more talk in pharmacist and confectionery circles than anything since the Smith Brothers sold their razors. He had not been able to get any very definite dope about the distribution plans, but it was common talk that Ribstone intended to spend half a million in the New York newspapers. He had heard that the Gray Matter Advertising Agency was to handle the account. Mr. O'Keefe said that Mr. Gray was an old friend of his, but going to Gray's office to inquire he found the reception room so choked with solicitors from the newspapers that he did not wait.

Mr. Oldham asked if this man Ribstone had had previous experience in the drug specialty line which would warrant their believing he could make a go of the so-called Ginger Cubes.

Mr. Gartenbaum said that Ribstone had had no experience in that field, so far as he knew, but that he was a very clever merchandiser and had done big

The Story of Ginger Cubes

things with the Ribstone Memory Course several years
ago.

Professor Devonshire of the laboratory department
was called upon to ask if he had any idea what the
formula of the Ginger Cubes might be, and whether it
could be easily duplicated or improved. Professor
Devonshire said that, speaking as a chemist, ginger
had many possibilities as a popular drug staple, that its
principal constituents are starch, volatile oil, and resin;
that it has carminative and purgative values, especially
for dyspepsia and flatulence, and is helpful for seasick-
ness, headache, and toothache. He said that as soon
as the Cubes themselves were on the market he could
analyze them and suggest a variation in the formula.

Mr. O'Keefe said that he had tried to get hold of
some of the Cubes, but that they were being carefully
kept under cover. He believed that Ribstone's plans
were still in the air until his advertising man, Russell,
was out of hospital.

Mr. Gartenbaum asked if Mr. Russell was in hos-
pital because he had been trying some of the Ginger
Cubes.

Mr. Oldham said that he had been greatly impressed
by the amount of gossip in the trade about the Ginger
Cubes, but he believed the value of the thing lay not
in any unique formula but in the cleverness of the name
Ginger Cubes, and particularly the additional name
Digestive Dice.

Mr. Gartenbaum agreed and submitted it to the
meeting that it would be well worth while to ride on
Ribstone's effort by putting out a similar product

The Powder of Sympathy

with an equally catchy name. He instanced the way
Eskimo Pie was followed immediately by a dozen imi-
tations, all very nearly as successful.

Mr. Sombre of the Promotion Department asked if
Mr. Gartenbaum had thought of any name as appealing
as Ginger Cubes.

Mr. Gartenbaum admitted he hadn't, but said that
his mind was working on this matter and the only
thing he had thought of so far was Ginger Blocks.

Mr. Sombre said he thought that was too similar
to Ginger Cubes and might mean legal proceedings.

Mr. O'Keefe suggested Tingling Squares.

After a good deal of discussion, Mr. Gartenbaum ad-
journed the meeting, ordering these minutes to be sent
confidentially to heads of departments. Another con-
ference to be held to-morrow at which suggestions for a
rival name would be brought in.

By E. K. R.,
Stenographer.

VII

[*A letter from Allan Russell, Advertising Manager of
the Ginger Cubes Corporation, to Nicholas Ribstone.*]

Hippocrates Hospital, April 14.

DEAR BOSS, I'm still a bit seedy but am getting better
every minute thanks to the care these "good people"
have taken of me. This is my first letter and it will
have to be short. Just wanted to say that if you still
need an assistant in the office I'd like to recommend
Miss Cumnor, one of the nurses here, who has been

The Story of Ginger Cubes

taking care of me. She is tired of the nursing job and wants to get into a "business position." Certainly she's a mighty capable girl and her medical knowledge would be of great value to us in marketing the Cubes. She is 23 years old and ambitious.

I'll be out of here pretty soon now, I hope, and am keen to get into the thick of the fight for the good old Cubes.

Yours always

Russell.

VIII

[A letter from Nicholas Ribstone to Allan Russell.]

Ginger Cubes Corporation

Nicholas Ribstone,
  President.
Theodore Carbo,
  Vice-President.
Arthur MacCready,
  Treasurer.
Simon Haggard,
  Secretary.
Allan Russell,
  Advertising Mgr.

Executive Offices
2216 Duane Street
New York

Cable Address:
Gincubes

April 14, 1922.

Dear Russell: Here are our letterheads. How do you like them? I am sending some to the hospital so you can use them for any letters you may need to write. Show them to the nurses and get their reaction. The more they circulate, the better.

This is just to tell you that I am going out of town for a little rest over the week-end. We have got things pretty well lined up so far. I shall be glad when you get back so we can visit together for I want your advice. You understand advertising men better

[165]

than I do, I guess. To me, a great deal of their jargon
is a mystery. What, for instance, do you think of the
enclosed one that 'has just come to me from the Gray
Matter Agency? Does it mean anything?

Miss Balboa, by the way, is somewhat upset by a
remark made by your Miss Cumnor, about our error
in spelling the name of the Hospital. I'm afraid the
mistake was due to my wrong pronunciation, which
she misunderstood.

As ever,

NICHOLAS RIBSTONE.

N.R./D.B.
(Encl.)

IX

*[Enclosure, sent by Mr. Ribstone to Mr. Russell, being a
letter from the Gray Matter Advertising Agency.]*

MY DEAR MR. RIBSTONE: Obviously you intend,
ultimately at any rate, to have a nation-wide, or even
world-wide, distribution for the Ginger Cubes. You
are going to need a large merchandising staff. I wish
to enlist your interest in our newly created Department
of Salesmanizing. Let us train your representatives
before they go on the road, and instil into the personnel
just those qualities of enthusiasm and confidence that
go to make not mere salesmen, but Ambassadors of
Commerce.

I solicit the pleasure of convincing you on this topic;
in the meantime let me briefly state the nutshell of our
theory.

In our Salesmanizing School, which is really a kind of

[166]

The Story of Ginger Cubes

Graduate College of the Selling Arts, we seek to drive out from the student all negative and minus thoughts, ideas of possible failure, business depression, etc., and to substitute robust energizing concepts, positive and plus in their nature. Many a man has come to us doubtful about his own selling abilities, doubtful about the general condition of trade, doubtful about economics and literature and even theology. When they leave us, after a three weeks' course under Mr. Harvey K. Tidaholm, they have pronounced convictions.

You wish to have your product—the Ginger Cubes —marketed swiftly, cleanly, universally. There are four steps in this process. The commodity must be

(1) Institutionalized
(2) Publicized
(3) Distributionized
(4) Internationalized

To bring this about, your representative personnel must be

(a) Humanized ⎫
(b) Stabilized ⎬ = SALESMANIZED
(c) Energized ⎭

It is on such matters as these that Consumer Preference and Dealer Convictionability are based.

I should like very much to have our Mr. Harvey K. Tidaholm discuss this matter with you. I know that your reaction will be enthusiastic.

Yours faithfully,
GEO. W. GRAY,
Technical Director, Gray Matter Advertising Service.

The Powder of Sympathy

X

[A letter from Nicholas Ribstone to George W. Gray.]

DEAR MR. GRAY: I am just leaving town for a few days rest. All decisions have been postponized until my advertising manager returns. He is now hospitalized. I will confer with you as soon as I am re-urbanized.

Yours truly,
(Signed, in absence, with rubber stamp.)
NICHOLAS RIBSTONE.

N.R./D.B.

XI

[An article in LOZENGE AND PASTILLE, the weekly trade journal of the throat tablet trade.]

THE VALUE OF THE CUBICAL FORM FOR MEDICATED CANDIES

BY BEN F. MENTHOL,
Secretary of National Lozenge Men's Chamber of Commerce.

A great deal of talk has been roused in lozenge circles by the formation of the Ginger Cubes Corporation, to manufacture and distribute a new product called the Ginger Cubes. Mr. Nicholas Ribstone, the head of the enterprise, while reticent as to details, admits that he hopes to spring a surprise on the world of bronchial tablets and breath-perfumers. We understand that the Ginger Cubes, while more in the geneal nature of a confection than a medical preparation, are

[168]

The Story of Ginger Cubes

based on a careful pharmacal formula, and will go before the public on an appeal at least partly therapeutic.

But what interests us is, that Mr. Ribstone's venture again brings up the necessity of standardizing the shape of the medicated sweet, if lozenge men are ever to get back to genuine prosperity. At present the lozenge and jujube world is in a state of wild disorder and lack of intelligent coöperation. Post-war deflation has not been followed by anything constructive. Lozenge men are cutting one another's throats instead of healing the public's. Mr. Ribstone, unconsciously, has put his finger on a vital spot in the lozenge industry.

Hitherto the trade has manufactured its products mainly in four shapes:

(1) Square tablet
(2) Round tablet
(3) Spherical
(4) Oval

It will be evident, however, that for close packing and neat appearance, the cube is undoubtedly an attractive shape. It is well worth consideration on the part of the trade whether a general adoption of the cube would not be advantageous. Moreover, a great economy could be effected by standardizing cartons and containers. How can the present debilitating fluctuations be ironed out while the whole industry is proceeding on a basis of mere individualism? We do not wish to disparage competition, which is the life of trade, but to advocate a higher form of coöperating competition. The lozenge trade owes it as a duty to humanity to take

The Powder of Sympathy

its part in the general stabilizing and soothing movement. The inflamed throat of Commerce can never be healed until lozenge men get together. There is no reason why the breath-sweetener clique should be so jealous of the digestive wing, both suspicious of larynx and bronchial men. We hope that at the convention in June these matters can be taken up and constructively dealt with.

XII

[A letter from Mr. Gray of the Gray Matter Advertising Agency to Nicholas Ribstone, proprietor of the Ginger Cubes.]

MY DEAR MR. RIBSTONE: I do not wish to seem too insistent, but I am so interested in the success of the Ginger Cubes that I feel it is my duty to inform you of the tested methods in which prosperity has been attained by other manufacturers.

I am so confident of your eventually deciding to place your advertising account in our hands that I went ahead last week and had our Laboratory of Merchandising Survey conduct a preliminary clinic in the local field. Of course, you understand that you are not obligated in any way; but I felt that this was the most useful mode of helping you to envisage your problem.

Just a word about our Merchandising Survey work, which is headed by Mr. Henry W. Geniall. Mr. Geniall is a man who knows how to talk to dealers in their own language; he is a born sales engineer. He

The Story of Ginger Cubes

began selling in 1892 and has never stopped; though now he sells service instead of commodities. He is the author of a book which has run through fifteen editions, including the Scandinavian, entitled *How to Meet and Dominate Your Fellow Men*, an autographed copy of which I am having forwarded to you.

The principle of our Merchandising Survey is to conduct a preliminary investigation of markets, in a representative field and on the highest plane of detached observation. Our Merchandising Surveyors are not to be confused with the street men employed by the less professional agencies. Most of them are college graduates; they are so tactful and genteel that they are welcomed by the dealers as valuable counsellors and coöperators; very often they are asked to stay to supper.

The survey we conducted shows conclusively that there is going to be a big market for Ginger Cubes if they are well publicized. We drew up the inclosed printed blank and questionnaired 100 druggists in the uptown section, just as a preliminary test. I have selected the inclosed at random from the returns, to show you the kind of thing. The others are being bound in a folder, which I will have much pleasure to lay before you on your return to the office, together with a tabulated analysis.

It is a pleasure to be able to put at your disposal all the resources of Gray Matter Service.

Faithfully yours,

GEO. W. GRAY.

Technical Director, Gray Matter Advertising Service.

[171]

The Powder of Sympathy

XIII

[Confidential Report of an interview with a druggist by a Merchandising Surveyor from the Gray Matter Advertising Agency.]

INTERVIEW

Name—Higgly-Piggly Drug Store.
Address—673 Sunnyside Ave.
Type of Store—Chain.
Party Interviewed—J. K. Liquorice, Mgr.
Subject of Interview—Ginger Cubes Canvass.
Approachtalk Used—General Coöperation No. 3, as per Mr. Geniall's suggestion.

What Brands of the following Does Dealer Sell—
(List in order of popularity):
Throat Tablets—Roko, Southern Soothers, Tussicules.
Cough Drops—Lady Larynx, Lotos Cone.
Confectionery Laxatives—Sugar Chew, Cascarilla.
Appetizer Lozenges—Paprika Pastilles, Curlicues.
Digestive Tablets—Stowaways, Cul de Sacs.
Medicated Candies—Sweeto, Spicy Chiplets, Candoids.
Breath Purifiers—Balmozone, Pineapple Hints, Clover Slices.

———

To What Does Dealer Attribute Success of These Best Sellers? Newspaper Advertising.
Does He Push Any Particular Brands? If so, Which? No Answer.

[172]

The Story of Ginger Cubes

What Methods of Manufacturers' Promotion Produces Best Result for the Dealer? Newspaper Advertising.

What per cent. of his customers suffer from Sore Throat? Ten per cent. in winter.

What per cent. from bad digestion? No answer.

What per cent. from cacopneumonia (bad breath)? No answer.

What per cent. prefer a doctor's prescription to a patent medicine? Fifty per cent.

What Does Dealer think of prospects of Ginger Cubes? Excellent; thinks name very "catchy."

Does Dealer approve the subtitle "Digestive Dice"? Yes.

Will He Use Window Display Material? Sure.

General Remarks—Dealer suggests we investigate what effect the Ginger Cubes will have on smokers' tongue; says ginger bites the tongue after smoking, would not have percentage of ginger too powerful.

Name of Surveyor—Richmond Brown.

Analyzed by Henry W. Geniall.

XIV

[A letter from Allan Russell, Advertising Manager of the Ginger Cubes Corporation, to his employer, Mr. Nicholas Ribstone.]

Hippocrates Hospital, April 18.

DEAR BOSS: This is just to say that I am so much better I expect to get out of here in a few days, and hope to be back "on the job" next week. Dr. Nichevo says that I have made surprising progress and

The Powder of Sympathy

thinks it is due to Miss Cumnor's fine care. She is
certainly some nurse. She and I have gone over those
papers you sent me, from the Gray Matter people,
very carefully. Miss Cumnor's reaction is that we
ought to go slow about signing up with them. She
thinks, and I am inclined to agree with her, that they
talk tripe. By the way, you didn't reply to my sug-
gestion about our giving her a job in the office. She is
certainly a remarkable woman.

Yours always,

RUSSELL.

XV

[*A letter from Mr. Nicholas Ribstone to his secretary,
Miss Daisy Balboa.*]

Kill Kare Kountry Klub,
Wayanda, Conn., April 18.

DEAR MISS BALBOA: I have decided to stay here a
few days longer for the fishing. Nothing much can be
done in the office until Mr. Russell returns, and it just
happens that one of the big drug jobbers is staying at
this place and it will do no harm for me to get to know
him in a social way. Thanks for telling me about the
Gray Matter portfolio. I am interested to know that
you are impressed by their enthusiasm. But every one
is enthusiastic when they go out fishing for a big one.

Look here, instead of mailing the Gray Matter stuff,
why not run up here with it yourself? I will get you
a reservation at the Bonhomie Inn, which is near this
club, and then we can go over the papers together.
There's a train that leaves Grand Central at 4:20.

The Story of Ginger Cubes

The little change would do you good, and there are several matters on which I wish to get your reaction.

Sincerely yours,

NICHOLAS RIBSTONE.

XVI

[A letter from Miss Balboa to Mr. Russell.]

DEAR MR. RUSSELL: Mr. Ribstone is still away, but I am going up to the country this afternoon to take him some papers, including your letter of yesterday. We'll all be mighty glad to see you when you get back.

Faithfully yours,

DAISY BALBOA.

XVII

[A letter from Mr. Gray, of Gray Matter Service, to Mr.' Ribstone, proprietor of the Ginger Cubes.]

MY DEAR MR. RIBSTONE: I was glad to get your note from Kill Kare Kountry Klub, and to hear that you have been taking a few days' recreation. You will return, I am confident, much refreshed and eager to take up the problems that confront us.

I have been a little disappointed at not getting a definite authorization from you to go ahead with our plans. We have had tentative advances from other possible clients in this same general field, but I have put them off, desiring not to take on any accounts that might possibly conflict with the Ginger Cubes. To be perfectly frank, the thing that has appealed to me about Ginger Cubes is the bully opportunity for public service in a big way, and the chance to institutionalize a prod-

The Powder of Sympathy

uct whose possibilities have filled the members of our organization with unusual enthusiasm.

Ever since we first began talking institutional advertising for Ginger Cubes, a real thought impression has been epitomizing itself in my mind, and our Department of Cumulative Service has been giving the matter special study and analytical constructive investigation. We have been going right back to fundamentals on this proposition, studying the different sides of the problem along all its different angles. It will indeed be a source of satisfaction if we are accorded the opportunity to work with you. Our Mr. Geniall was saying in conference yesterday, "I am convinced I would rather be associated with the Ginger Cubes Corporation than any other company I know of, because what I have heard of the quality of men that make up that organization and the quality of service they would expect convinces me it would be an educative experience to coöperate with that firm. The product-attributes of their Ginger Cubes fill me with enthusiasm, and I feel that if they were our clients we could work for them as personal friends, and not in any cold-blooded businesslike fashion."

That is the way we want you, Mr. Ribstone, to feel towards our organization.

It is not our desire to merely build a number of advertisements which may be combined together in a more or less connected series by some such device as art treatment. Art is all very well as a handmaiden of advertising, but for a monumental campaign you need the inspiration of a Big Idea, a genuinely dominating thought that will clarionize every piece of copy and tie the whole together in a culminating increment of public consciousness.

Advertising is either Product-Advertising or Institutional-Advertising. The functions of the first are obvious—

A. Function is to sell product
B. Means of accomplishment are
    (1) Directly presenting the product to the market
    (2) Urging the market to accept the product

But Institutional-Advertising is far more psychological. Here enters the supreme function of the merchandising arts, to create consumer "good-will." This may be defined as encouraging consumer-benevolence, that is, educating the public to a sense of subjective interest in the entire business, and a conscious awareness of benefit therefrom. A feeling of friendly satisfaction engendered by Knowledge, Understanding and Appreciation is the inception of this consumer-benevolence.

The various factors that jointly and severally enter into these great merchandising truths I will not insist upon. But it would give me great satisfaction if you and Mr. Russell would meet the members of our organization and talk the whole matter over frankly and fully. Mr. Russell and your good self and the writer ought to get together in the near future for a long, serious talk on the whole proposition. We could not do nearly so well for you if our headquarters were not in New York, where we can have daily intimate con-

The Powder of Sympathy

ference with your organization headquarters. Our psychological director for the Chicago Territory, Mr. Alfred Ampere, has been so stimulated by what he has heard of your plans, that he wires me asking to be transferred to New York if our proposition goes through. I am inclined to favour appointing him as chief contact man, so that he could be summoned at any time within twenty minutes if a conference were called.

The objectives are all clearly defined, and we are ready to go to work. This is simply to assure you of my own personal appreciation of the splendid energy and fighting spirit your organization exhibits, and to hope that from the very inception of the Ginger Cubes we may be accorded an opportunity to coöperate in the public educationalization which is the real satisfaction of the advertising profession.

Cordially yours,

GEO. W. GRAY.

Technical Director, Gray Matter Advertising Agency.

XVIII

[*Story in the New York Lens, April 23, written by the star humorous reporter.*]

CUPID COMES TO DOCTORS' AID

HOSPITAL ROMANCE CULMINATES
IN PATIENT WEDDING
PRETTY NURSE

Allan Russell, advertising man, left Hippocrates Hospital yesterday afternoon, completely cured of a

The Story of Ginger Cubes

stubborn case of nervous debility that at first puzzled the doctors. With him, in a taxicab, was Miss Candida Cumnor, one of the nurses, still in her uniform. They went to the Little Church Around the Corner and were married. After the ceremony, Mrs. Russell took her husband's temperature with a clinical thermometer. It was Centigrade A, or whatever the normal reading is. She did not test his pulse, which was probably excusably fluttered. Even a hardened reporter, who horned in on this story by accident, was stirred by the sight of the bride in her crisp white linen. She has golden-bronzy hair and indigo eyes, or they looked that way in the twilight of the church. But what's the use? She is now Mrs. Russell.

During Mr. Russell's illness Miss Candida had charge of the case. She sympathized with his business problem—Dr. Nichevo, the Hippocrates expert on nervous mechanics, said that he had been run down by too constant intercourse with advertising agencies. She took his temperature soothingly with that cold little glass tube. But what she took away with one hand she gave back with the other. When her palm floated like a water-lily across his commerce-heated brow his mind grew calm, but his heart was caloric. As he became stronger she assisted him with advertising layouts which were spread on the bed, and they pored over them together. Why is it, we wonder, that reporters never have time to be taken ill?

Mr. Russell is Advertising Manager of the Ginger Cubes Corporation. He and his wife expect to spend their honeymoon hunting an apartment.

The Powder of Sympathy

"Cupid is the best doctor," said Mr. Russell as they left the church. "I intend to keep the thermometer as a souvenir."

XIX

[A letter from Nicholas Ribstone, proprietor of the Ginger Cubes, to Allan Russell.]

Bonhomie Inn, April 23.

DEAR RUSSELL: Forgive my delay in writing, but I have exciting news for you. Miss Balboa and I have decided to get married. You know that I have always felt we laboured under a handicap in not being able to get disinterested feminine reaction on the Cubes. Miss Balboa's excellent sense will be a great help. I dare say you will be surprised—I am, myself. I had thought I was too old to become a Benedictine, but Miss Balboa has quite carried me off my feet. I must not be sentimental, however. We are going to be married here, to-morrow, very quietly.

I should have written to you before about Miss Cumnor. I thought rather well of your suggestion, but Miss Balboa has convinced me that it is better not to add to our staff just now, at any rate until we get things going.

I'm sending this to the office, as I guess you have left the hospital by now. Mr. and Mrs. Nicholas Ribstone will be back in a few days.

Yours always,
NICHOLAS RIBSTONE.

The Story of Ginger Cubes

XX

[Another letter from Mr. Ribstone.]

Bonhomie Inn, April 24.

DEAR RUSSELL: Just got your wire. Congratulations. It reaches me on the brink of the altar myself. My Lord, man, you should have tipped me off beforehand. It wasn't necessary for both of us to get married in order to get wifely reactions on the Cubes. If I had known sooner—but anyhow, it's all arranged now.

Miss Balboa has just about convinced me that we will do well to accept Gray Matter's proposition. I wish I could consult you about this. Perhaps you had better get in touch with Gray and have the papers ready for signing when I get to the office.

We can exchange wedding presents later on. At the moment I'm too flustered to know just what happens next.

Yours, from the jumping-off place,
NICHOLAS RIBSTONE.

XXI

[A letter from Allan Russell to an old friend, known to us only as Bob.]

DEAR BOB: There's the devil to pay in this office. I've just heard that old Ribstone has married Miss Balboa, his stenographer, in order to get her unbiassed reactions on business. Now I know very well that Candida and Mrs. Balboa-Ribstone will never get on together. This Balboa person, for instance, has argued old Rib into believing that the Gray Matter stuff is real. Candida doesn't fall for it, says it's the bunk. I won't go on as Ad. Mgr. if Ribstone accepts the Gray Matter contract. I just want to ask you if there's anything in your office that I could take a hand in. You know my experience and qualifications. Let me have a line.

Yrs. in haste,

A. R.

XXII

[*An editorial in LOZENGE AND PASTILLE.*]

We hear that Nicholas Ribstone, of the Ginger Cubes Corporation, has sold out his entire interest in the much-touted Cubes to the National Drug Novelties Company. This comes as quite a surprise to the trade, as no specialty in recent years had aroused so much advance interest as the Ginger Cubes. The figure paid by National Drug Novelties for the formula, stock in hand, and jobbing contracts already arranged, is said to be half a million dollars. We await with interest to hear just how Gartenbaum and his associates will develop this property. In the meantime the affair suggests some meditations on the desirability of guarding the medicated confectionery industry against the machinations of mere adventurers and speculators.

(Walk, Not Run,
to Nearest Exit)

[182]

THE EDITOR AT THE BALL GAME
(WORLD'S SERIES OPENING, 1922)

A T THE Polo Grounds yesterday $119,000 worth of
baseball was played. Of that, however, only a
meagre $60,000 or so went to the players. We wonder
how much the accumulated sports writers got for writ-
ing about it. They are the real plutocrats of pro-
fessional athletics.

We have long intimated our inflexible determination
to learn how to be a sports writer—or, as he is usually
called, a Scribe. This is to announce progress. We
are getting promoted steadily. In the 1920 World's
Series we were high up in the stand. At the Dempsey-
Carpentier liquidation we were not more than a para-

The Powder of Sympathy

sang from the ring.   We broke into the press box at the 1921 World's Series, but only in the rearward allotments assigned to correspondents from Harrisburg and Des Moines.

But our stuff is beginning to be appreciated.   We are gaining.   Yesterday we found ourself actually below the sacred barrier—in the Second Row, right behind the Big Fellows.   Down there we were positively almost on social terms (if we had ventured to speak to them) with chaps like Bill McGeehan and Grant Rice and Damon Runyon and Ring Lardner.   Well, there are a lot of climbers in the world of sporting literature.

One incident amused us.   We heard a man say, "Which one is Damon Runyon?"   "Over there," said another, pointing.   The first, probably hoping to wangle some sort of prestige, made for Mr. Runyon.   "Hullo, Damon!" he cried genially.   "Remember me?"

It must have been Pythias.

So far we have only been allowed to shoot in a little preliminary patter—what managing editors call "human interest stuff."   When the actual game starts they take the wire away from us, quite rightly, and turn it over to the experts.   But, being inexorably ambitious, we sit down now, after the game is over, to tell you exactly how we saw it.   Because we had a unique opportunity to study a great journalist and see exactly how it's done.   It was just our good luck, sitting in the second row.   The second sees better than the first— it's higher.   You have to use your knee for writing desk, and you have to pull up your haunches every few minutes to let by the baseball editor of the Topeka *Clarion*

The Editor at the Ball Game

on his way back to Harry Stevens's Gratis Tiffin for another platter of salad. But the second row gave us our much needed opportunity to watch the leaders of our craft.

It was just before the game began. The plump lady in white tights (a little too opulent to be Miss Kellermann, but evidently a diva of some sort) was about to begin the walking race around the bases against the athletic-looking man. She won, by the way—what a commutrix she would make. Suddenly we recognized a very Famous Editor climbing into the seat directly in front of us. He was followed by two earnest young men. One of these respectfully placed a Noiseless typewriter in front of the Editor, and spread out a thick pile of copy paper.

This young man had shell spectacles and truncated side-whiskers. Both young men were plainly experts, and were there to tell the Editor the fine points of what was happening. The Famous Editor's job was to whale it out on the Noiseless, with that personal touch that has made him (it has been said) the most successful American newspaper man.

This, we said to ourself, is going to be better than any Course in Journalism.

We admired the Editor for the competent business-like way he went to work. He wasted no time in talking. After one intent glance round through very brightly polished spectacles, he began to tick—to "file," as we professionals say. Already, evidently, he felt the famous "reactions" coming to him. He looked so charmingly scholarly, like some well-loved

The Powder of Sympathy

college professor, we could not help feeling it was just a little sad to see him taking all this so seriously. He never paused to enjoy the scene (it really is a great sight, you know), but pattered along on the keys like a well-trained engine.

The two young men fed him facts; with austere and faintly indignant docility he turned these into the well-known pseudo-philosophic comment. It was beautifully efficacious. The shining, well-tended typewriter, the plentiful supply of smooth yellow paper, the ribbon printing off a clear blue, these were right under our eyes; we couldn't help seeing the story rolling out though most of the time we averted our eyes in a kind of shame. It seemed like studying the nakedness of a fine mind.

"Jack Dempsey's coming in," said the young man. Or, "Babe Ruth at bat." The Editor was too busy to look up often. One flash of those observant (and always faintly embittered, we thought) eyes could take in enough to keep the mind revolving through many words. "I'll take them, and correct the typographical errors," remarked young Shellspecs, gathering up the Editor's first page. Thereafter the Editor passed over his story in "takes" and young Shellspecs copyread it with a blue pencil. Once the Editor said, a little tartly: "Don't change the punctuation." From Shellspecs the pages went smoothly to the silent telegraph operator who sat between them.

Our mind—if we must be honest—was somewhat divided between admiration and pity. Here, indeed, is slavery, we said to ourself, watching the great man

The Editor at the Ball Game

bent over his work. Babe Ruth came to the plate. Judge Landis is named after a mountain, but Ruth looks like one. There was pleasant dramatic quality in the scene: the burly, gray figure swinging its bat, the agile and dangerous-looking Mr. Nehf winding up for delivery, the twirl of revolving arms against a green background, the flashing, airy swim of the ball, the turbine circling of the bat, the STRIKE sign floating silently upon the distant scoreboard . . . but did the Editor have time to savour all this? Not he! One quick wistful peer upward through those clear lenses, he was back again on his keyboard—the Noiseless keyboard carrying words to the noisiest of papers.

And yet, we had to insist, here was also genius of a sort. The swiftness with which he translated it all into a rude, bright picture! But he was going too consciously on high, we thought. Proletarianizing it, fitting the scene into his own particular scheme of thinking, instead of genuinely puzzling out its suggestions. He was honest enough to admit that the game itself was mostly rather dull—and in so far he was much above most of the Sporting Writers, those high-spirited lads who come back from a quite peaceable game and lead you to believe that there have been scenes of thunder and earthquake.

But, like most of us, he tended to exaggerate those things he had decided upon beforehand. He made much of the roaring of the crowd—which, after all, was not violent as crowds go; and he wrote cheerily of the bitterness of hatred manifested towards the umpires, the deadly glances of players questioning close

[187]

The Powder of Sympathy

decisions. He seemed to view these matters through a pupil dilated with intellectual belladonna (if that's what belladonna does).

He wrote something about the perfect happiness of the small boy who was the Giant mascot. Heaven, he said, would have to be mighty good to be better than this for that urchin. But to us the boy seemed totally calm, even sombre. What does baseball mean to him? More interesting, and more exact, we thought, would have been to note the fluctuating sounds of the spectators; a constant rhythm of sound and silence—the hush as the pitcher winds up, the mixed surge of comment as the ball flicks across, the sudden unanimous outcry at some dramatic stroke. Or the ironical cadenced clapping and stamping that break out spontaneously at certain recognized moments of suspense.

But the Editor was going strong, and we felt a kind of admiring affection for him as we saw him so true to form. He picked reactions out of the ether, hit them square on the nose, and whaled them to Shellspecs. Shellspecs recorded faultless assists, zooming them in to Western Union.

In the third inning the Editor hoisted a paragraph clean over the heads of the bleachers by quoting the Bible. Mr. Bush, the red-sleeved Yankee pitcher, was at bat and lifted a midfield fly. Bancroft made a superb tergiversating catch going at full speed. It was beautifully done.

For the second time, we thought, history has been made in America by a Bancroft. "The human body is a wonderful machine," ticked the busy Editor. We

The Editor at the Ball Game

watched Mr. Bancroft more carefully after that. A small agile fellow, there was much comeliness in the angle of his trunk and hips as he leaned forward over the plate, preparing for the ball.

In the fourth inning the Editor was already at page 13 of his copy. The young man with truncated side-whiskers then drew the rebuke for inserting commas into the story. The other young man, sitting behind, kept volleying bits of Inside Stuff. Scott came to bat. "This fellow," said Inside Stuff, "is known as the Little Iron Man; he's played in one thousand consecutive games." This was faithfully relayed to the Editor by Shellspecs, and went into the story. But the Editor changed it to "almost a thousand." This pleased us, for we also felt a bit skeptical about that item.

By this time, having noted the quickness of the Editor at "reactionizing," we were very keen to get something of our own into his story. An airplane came over. Inside Stuff announced that the plane was taking pictures to be delivered in Cleveland in time for the morning papers. How he knew this, we can't guess—very likely he didn't. This also faithful Shellspecs passed on. The plane was a big silvery beauty —we remarked, loudly, to our neighbour that she looked as though made of aluminum. A moment later the Editor, having handed a page to Shellspecs, said: "Add that the plane was aluminum." Shellspecs wrote down in blue pencil: "It's an aluminum flying machine." But we mustn't be unjust. Very likely the Editor got the reaction just as we did. It was fairly obvious.

The Powder of Sympathy

Sixth Inning—The Editor hit a hot twisting paragraph to the outposts of his syndicate, but troubled Shellspecs by saying—Mr. Whitey Witt's name having been mentioned—"Is he a Yankee or a Giant?" "He's an albino, has pink eyes," volunteered indefatigable Inside Stuff. The flying keys caught it and in it went, somewhat philosophized: "Lack of pigment in hair, skin, and retina seems not to diminish his power." Inside Stuff: "It's the beginning of the Seventh and they're all stretching. It's the usual thing." But no stretching for the Editor. He goes on and on. Twenty pages now. When his assistants put a fact just where he likes it his quick mind knocks it for five million circulation.

"Stengel, considered a very old man in baseball," says the cheery mentor. "He's thirty-one years old." To none of these suggestions does the Editor make any comment. He wastes no words—orally, at least. He knows what he wants—sifts it instanter.

We left at the end of the Eighth. The Editor was still going strong. He didn't see the game, but we think he was happy in his own way.

We hope we haven't seemed too impertinent. We want to be a Scribe—not a Pharisee. But our interest in the profession is greater than our regard for any merely individual sanctity. We've given you a faithful picture of what has been called supreme success in journalism. Take a good look at it, you students of newspapers, and see how you like it. We'll tell you a secret. It's pretty easy, if that's the sort of thing you hanker for. In a way, it's rather thrilling. But (between ourselves) it's also a Warning.

THE DAME EXPLORES WESTCHESTER

WE FEAR that the Salamis dealer in cigars, news-
papers, and ice cream cones thinks we are a low-
spirited fellow. For ten days or so preceding the
Fourth of July he urged us every day not to forget to
buy our supply of firecrackers from him. Finally he
grew so insistent that we had to tell him the truth. We
don't believe in firecrackers for small children, we told
him. Well, how about some nice rockets, balloons,
Roman candles? he cried. No, we said firmly; Mr.
Mackay, up on Harbour Hill, shoots off about five
thousand dollars' worth of very lovely fireworks every
Fourth of July evening for the pleasure of the villagers;
why should we attempt vainly to compete?

But of course, something had to be done to celebrate
the Fourth. It would be only just, we thought, to have
an adventure that would give pleasure to Dame
Quickly, who has given us more innocent cheer than
any one else during the past year. Besides, she had
just attained the dignity of having travelled more than
8,000 miles. Excepting for two or three tentative and
brief excursions upon Manhattan, she had never been

The Powder of Sympathy

off Long Island. We had heard, from time to time, that across the Sound there lay a region of mystery and heyday called Westchester County—a land supposed to be more aristocratic and splendid than anything our lowly Paumanok could show. A land, they said, flowing with gasolene and Eskimo Pie. But, in our timid and non-temerarious disposition we had never ventured. The ferry from Sea Cliff to New Rochelle ceased running during the war and has never resumed. The ferry from Oyster Bay to Greenwich—well, we had once made inquiry as to the prices; 25 cents per foot, measured over all, for the vehicle alone, to say nothing of the fare for the occupants. But, then, we had heard rumour of a humbler craft plying between College Point and The Bronx. This, we had an instinctive prompting, would be the caper. We determined to make the attempt.

No one has yet (so far as we know) properly uttered the fine poetry of a car that feels herself turned loose for the day upon unknown paths. That strong, rigorous hum underneath the bonnet, the intelligent questing look of her hood as it goes snouting along the road—these are potent mystery. The Younger Generation, duly caparisoned for either shine or rain, were installed, and ejaculated innocent defiance. Two small and quite useless wooden rabbits accompanied them, emblems of fortune and also of the Occupational Therapy Society (from whom they were purchased). The Urchin and Urchiness were hopeful of storm; they enjoy seeing a parent hustle to rig up the curtains. Some day we shall fool them by getting a sedan. We

The Dame Explores Westchester

have a name already chosen for her. She will be Diana of the Crossways. The Microcosm, still too young to care what happens to her, was a nugget of plump, regardless cheer. Titania wore her khaki breeks, which are astoundingly comely. This had all the earmarks of a Foray against Relentless Destiny.

So, without hap—save for two grievous motor-bikers near Willets Point, who had jammed their clutch and halted the Dame to beg the borrow of a screwdriver— the equipage proceeded mildly to College Point. Here there was secret applause when the official said that only 50 cents would be necessary. That excellent ancient vessel the *Steinway* was already waiting. The Dame, with an air of skittish enterprise, trundled aboard. Befitting a boat of such orchestral name, a person with the word *Musician* embroidered on his cap played a powerful concertina. Already it seemed a literary excursion, for the chauffeur, studying his map, learned that not far away was a region of The Bronx called Casanova. Let this be a reminder, he said to himself, to read the frequently but enigmatically commended memoirs of De Seingalt. The chevalier himself, it is said, was once reduced to playing a fiddle in a cabaret: perhaps this concertina person is also a virtuoso of quality in an ad interim embarrassment. In the brass bowl ingeniously affixed to the machine of melody the chauffeur contributed a nickel as cautious largesse to Art.

On such occasions, adventuring in little-known parts of this great panorama of surprise known as New York, we reflect sadly on our own lack of enterprise in ex-

The Powder of Sympathy

ploring its grim hilarities. Indeed we always intend to spend all our time on the streets, where we are endlessly happy and entertained; it is only a lack-lustre and empty resolution towards answering letters that brings us to the office. By this time, however, the *Steinway* had reached Clason Point, and with a keen sense of excitement we set forth to examine new lands and strange.

The first thing to do was to lay in some lunch. On Westchester Avenue our eye was caught by the sign *Bible & Son, Undertakers and Real Estate;* right next door was a meritorious-looking delicatessen shop, which we invaded. The young man in charge was much pleased. All his family had gone away for a three days' holiday and had left him to run the store; the Fourth was proving shockingly tranquil, he said; he was so gratified by getting our trade that he gave us a bottle opener for the near-beer. We thought we were doing very well in our purchasing when Titania entered and revised it, saying that sardines would not do for the Younger Generation. Turning north at a venture, we found the Williamsbridge Road, where lunch was enjoyed beside a damp, quiet woodland.

But it was after lunch, when we turned into the Boston Post Road, that the real thrills began. On that famous highway Dame Quickly seemed to feel herself really in swell company. But we were glad we had not attempted it in our freshman days as a driver. Off in the distance we could see Long Island, a quiet, blue profile: how calm it looked. A vast vanload of elated coloured folk, packed ecstatically on lurching camp

The Dame Explores Westchester

stools, groaned uphill on low gear. All subsequent traffic was stalled by this vehicle's sudden halt, and we found an impulsive flivver browsing along our fender. We began to wonder whether Westchester was as élite as they had told us. We were startled, also, by the number of kennels offering chows and those animals called Pekingese. We were glad Gissing had not accompanied us: we fear his hardy, vulgar soul would have scoffed.

New Rochelle seemed an almost unnecessarily large town; much larger than Long Islanders are used to. Larchmont is evidently very civilized. In Mamaroneck, when we sought the waterfront, we found ourself embarrassingly arriving at the front door of a private mansion. On such occasions Dame Quickly, who is really a very noble creature, looks suddenly paltry and shameful. We turned towards home, though we were sorry to leave the view of the rocks called SCOTCH CAPS. These appealed to all our instincts as a printer. And by the way: the low tide seems to go much lower over there than it does along Paumanok. Real estate men, we are told, always take care to bring their clients out that way at high water.

Titania had an eagerness to see Neptune Avenue in New Rochelle, where she had lived as an urchin. She hadn't been there for more than twenty years and said it was much changed. Trying to discover which had been the house, we found one for sale, and the door yielded to pressure. Inside, in an empty room, was a gilt sword blazoned with emblems of the Knights of Pythias or the Knights Templars or something of that

The Powder of Sympathy

sort. Somehow this seemed like an ideal setting for a humorous mystery story. We hoped that a crime had been committed; and yet the sword was very blunt.

We are still a confirmed Long Islander.

THE POWER AND THE GLORY

DEAR old Dr. Johnson used to pray to be delivered from "vacillation and vagrancy of mind, mental vellications and revulsions." These are also our most painful infirmity. The conflict of ambitions in the mind is no easy problem. When one considers the career of a man like Lord Northcliffe it is fairly evident that he knew more or less clearly what he wanted, and went after it. He wanted to be a Great Newspaper Proprietor, and he wanted to be a figure behind the scenes (but the scenes need not be too opaque) in politics. He succeeded very powerfully in all this, as competent and dogged men do when they have a clearly defined objective. And in order to succeed in this

The Powder of Sympathy

manner, it is fairly plain that he did not mind failure in the other realms of life. Poetry, peaceful privacy, philosophy, and all the other pensive pleasures that begin with a p, he was content (we imagine) to ignore.

This business of making up one's mind among the various ambitions that an exciting planet offers is highly perplexing. There is one part of our mind that hankers only for seclusion, rambling by lonely watersides, and plenty of ink and paper. There is another unregenerate lobe of our brain that would find a life of important trivial bustling like Northcliffe's highly diverting and agreeable. It must be interesting (we sometimes ponder) to have a steam yacht, play golf with Premiers, talk choppily and brusquely over the telephone to a hireling Editor, and persuade oneself that the great laws of life are coming to heel very nicely. There is no doubt about it, the business of being a Public Figure probably has in it a great deal of exhilarating excitement that keeps the mind from brooding and painful activity.

We were interested to read in one of the papers not long ago a piece about how a conscientious young man of wealth is studying to fit himself for "public life"— which means, presumably, politics. It would be profitable to hear a discussion from the local magi as to what constitutes the best training for a political career. Aristotle made some comment—didn't he?—about educating a special class of public servants—we must look it up in the *Politics*. We cannot rid ourself of the idea that the most important feature of such a training would be a considerable period of travel, to instil into

The Power and the Glory

the mind of the intending statesman that no one coun-
try has any monopoly of wisdom, humour, scenery, or
good cooking. We have been much struck by the fact
that since the war young graduates of British univer-
sities who would in earlier times have made their
Grand Tour on the mainland of Europe have been
trooping hither in astonishing numbers to have a look
at the American scene. It has evidently penetrated
the mind of the British political-minded classes that
social phenomena over here are important and interest-
ing enough to merit observation.

Almost every reasonably high-minded young man
has, we suppose, thought at one time or another about
the duty of going into politics—and then, if he has any
tincture of sensitiveness, has sheered off in alarm
after seeing the dreadful antics that the ambitious un-
derling has to perform. He has seen, perhaps, a cur-
rent event movie of an Assistant Secretary of the Navy
marching gayly in a parade of The Elks at Atlantic
City; or, driving quietly past a Long Island picnic
glade, has noticed a gathering in motor trucks—
Greenpoint Nest No. 653, Fraternal Order of Owls—
being harangued, preliminary to hot dogs and Eskimo
Pie, by a perspiring young man in white flannel trousers
who hopes for a job as Assemblyman. Do not mis-
understand us: we are not mocking these necessary
small jobs at the foot of the political ladder. They
have to be done, and it is only right that they should be
done by those zealous fellows who can get some fun
out of them. The life of politics, which we study with
increasing amazement, must be an exhausting and

The Powder of Sympathy

exciting one, very foreign to the placid instincts of the philosophic observer. The latter, if he is wise, will restrain his impulse to mock, and will try to preserve that mood of affectionate scrutiny which is the only permanently valuable attitude towards human affairs. But sometimes he will think that newspaper men ought to be drafted, by an occasional compulsory legislation, into Government service. After several years of unrebuked privilege to snap and snigger at public men the tables ought to be turned. Some of us who show, in our unmolested kennels, such sweet untested wisdom, might well be hounded out to take a share in the difficult, damnable business of making the machinery go. But the electorate need not be alarmed. There is no real danger. At the first tread on the stair the editor would be out by the window.

But we were speaking of Lord Northcliffe. We have never made a careful study of his career, but oddly enough we have always had a sort of sneaking affection for the man himself while regarding that type of person in general as extremely mischievous. We do not care at all for these people who accumulate newspapers much as they would a number of suits of clothes, and who hire editors to traipse round the world with them as a kind of subservient mouthpiece. We are being told by all the papers that Northcliffe "wielded terrific power." Well, in a way, we suppose he did; but it was a power that dealt mainly in ephemeral and unimportant things. Even his greatest triumph, the Premiership of Lloyd George, he could not permanently control. It was one of the oddities of coincidence that on the

The Power and the Glory

day of Northcliffe's death a cable dispatch comes in telling us that four of Mr. George's goats have won prizes at a goat show. Mr. George has a goat farm, it appears. If it would not seem heartless, we should say that Lord Northcliffe died rather than have to read Mr. Lloyd George's memoirs. He had a great spirit and a huge ambition; but we cannot see in his career any evidence that Public Life and power necessarily develop the finer and more sensitive parts of man.

GISSING JOINS A COUNTRY CLUB

A NUMBER of our clients have been asking for news of Haphazard Gissing, the Synthetic Dog. Since we have always been so candid with our patrons, we shall have to tell the unvarnished story of the latest surprising chapter in that romantic animal's career.

We say it with reluctance, and we say it with unfeigned sadness: we have had to deport Gissing. Admirable creature though he was, active, agile (you should have seen him play catch with a rubber ball), sonorous at night when he suspected alien footstep, highly intelligent and not devoid of a rude houndish comeliness—with all these gifts, he was not congenial among children. We do not know whether it was due to some dark strain of philosophy in him that rendered him too introspective to understand the ways of juveniles, or whether it was a blend of hot cavalier jealousy —at any rate, he never seemed able to unbend properly among the extremely young. The terror that he inspired in icemen and tinsmiths could be countenanced, but when he bristled and showed his teeth at neighbour-

Gissing Joins a Country Club

ing children something had to be done. It was the familiar problem of literature and life: here is an amiable creature, well beloved, possessed (by some kink of breeding) with an unexorcisable deviltry. We can leave it at that, and not harmonize the theme with sentimental arpeggios.

Of course the first thing to be done was to find a good home for the exile. We consulted Dr. Rothaug, the kindly veterinarian of Sea Cliff, at whose establishment Gissing took a cultural course last winter. Dr. Rothaug told us of a farmer in that pretty suburb of Glen Cove which is miscalled *Skunk's Misery*, who was said to be looking for a fierce watch-dog to guard his chickens. Thither we went, and found the farmer milking at a barn on the lonely hillside. But just the night before he had been given a tramp collie. We liked the look of the farm at Skunk's Misery; it was the kind of place where Gissing would have been well content, but the farmer said that one dog was enough. That night, very late, we let Gissing indoors, and shared a Last Supper with him at the icebox. Perhaps we shall remember that he seemed just a little surprised at the beef-bone and the arrowroot biscuits spread with Roquefort cheese. Well, we said to ourself defensively, he was always fond of Roquefort; there's only a scrap of it left; and very likely he'll never taste it again.

We refuse to be stampeded into any sentiment about this matter; we always thought that Gissing, as he matured, was developing a touch of the Thomas Hardy fatalism; he would be annoyed if we tried to over-dramatize this incident.

[203]

The Powder of Sympathy

The next day the whole family was mustered to pay
parting honours; all hands were embarked in Dame
Quickly; the condemned dog ate a hearty breakfast,
and with a bight of clothesline about his neck was
escorted to the chariot, his long unused hawser having
vanished since the Urchin used it to moor a full-rigged
ship to a neighbouring sapling. By this time the
victim had suspected something amiss; his deeply
stricken cider-coloured eye was painfully interrogative.
The Dame, however, seemed to us a trifle heartless.
Off she went, her cylinders drumming with their usual
alacritous smoothness. To a wedding or a funeral, all
one to her. Gissing, now probably reviewing inwardly
the tale of his errors (there must have been many of
which we are ignorant: we never did know where he
went on those long daily expeditions) was (we are
pleased to record it) too honourable to attempt any in-
sincere repentances. He kept climbing into the laps
of his guardians, but the ironist insists that this was
not all affection, but rather that the vibration of the
floorboards tickled his pads. There was an occasional
secret caress, both given and taken, but we know our
clients are too stiff in the bosom to want to hear about
such matters. The younger generation, in the back
seat, were eager to see the country club that Gissing
was going to join. So had the matter been explained
to them.

Across those autumn-tinted fields of central Long
Island—all colours of pink and fawn and panther with
the weathered shrivelling corn-shocks like old ghost-
Indian tepees, and the pumpkins bright in the stubble

Gissing Joins a Country Club

—we proceeded to the Bide-a-Wee Home, which lies tucked away in the woods near Wantagh. This place had been to us only a name, and indeed we knew not exactly what to expect. Great was our pleasure to find a charming old farmhouse with great barns and outhouses, and an immediate clamour from hundreds of dogs running gayly in fenced inclosures, and lesser dogs, both hale and cripple, about the yard. Gissing hopped out blithely: his tail lifted sharply over his back, feathering downward as it curved: the warm October air, one supposes, came to him sharply barbed with the aromas of innumerable congenials. He was very much alive, and walked nimbly on cushion toes. Holding the rope, we walked among the barns, saluted by prodigious applause from all sides. Even an inclosure full of cats showed gracious interest. The conclusion drawn by the Younger Generation was that Gissing's friends were glad to see him. Then came a genial curator, Gissing was led to a wire gate, and introduced into an orchard plot among about thirty more or less his own size. There was a good deal of bristling and growling, but he stood his ground calmly while a dozen or so of his new clubmates inquired into his credentials.

We had been somewhat troubled by the signboard of the Bide-a-Wee, which calls itself a *Home for Friendless Animals*. We wished to impress upon the curator that Gissing was far from friendless, but we soon found that the legend on the board was inaccurate. Many very well-loved animals go there, for one reason or another; the organization tries to find a suitable home

The Powder of Sympathy

for all the beasts in its care; the name and character-
istics of each are entered in a ledger when it arrives,
and, if he so desires, the previous owner is notified when
the animal goes to its new home. We were pleased to
learn also that much of the broken bread from the
Waldorf and Vanderbilt Hotels is shipped out to the
Bide-a-Wee; so, if you are lunching there and don't
finish your roll, perhaps Gissing will get it. (He is
particularly fond of the crescent-shaped ones, with little
black specks on them.) The Home is supported by
voluntary contribution. In the record book we in-
scribed Gissing's biography very briefly:

GISSING: *origin doubtful: two years old: has always
had a good home. A fine watch-dog, but not good with
children.*

We would have liked to go on, for much more might
have been said. We would have liked to tell the
friendly curator that this very week (by the quaint
irony of circumstance) a book is to be published of
which Gissing—somewhat transformed—is the hero.
But we thought it best not to mention this, lest it get
around among the other members and they taunt
Gissing about it. We were happy to leave him in so
congenial and friendly a home. And if any of our
clients happen to need a good dog for a lonely country
place—a dog who is perhaps too intellectual and ex-
citable for children, but a tocsin of excellent acoustic
strength—there you'll find him. He has promised to
write to the Urchiness, provided she eats her cereal a
little faster.

Gissing Joins a Country Club

As we left, Gissing was standing on his hind legs looking through the fence. He wailed just a little. It would be less than justice (to both sides) not to admit it. Like Milton's hero leaving the Garden, "a few natural tears he shed, but dried them soon." As the friendly curator said, "By to-morrow he'll think he's lived here all his life." On the way home, there being more room in the Dame, a supply of cider was laid in for consolation. Last night it seemed just a little strange to visit the icebox all alone. To-morrow, perhaps, we shall take lunch at the Waldorf.

THREE STARS ON THE BACK STOOP

BEFORE starting on our new notebook we have been looking over the old one. We are painfully astonished to see so many interesting ideas that we never turned to account.

We see no reason for being ashamed of using a memorandum book to jot down casual excitements in the mind. If you are really interested in what goes on inside your head, that is the only possible way to keep track of those flittermice of thought. Astronomers spend much time examining the Great Nebula in Orion, and other pinches of star dust that circumspangle the universe. It is equally important to scrutinize those dim patches of mental shining where, once in a while, one suspects the phosphorescent emergence of Truth. Unhappily, most of the ideas jotted down for sonnets and meditations never get anything done to them. They lie there unexercised, and once a year or so, when we run through the pile of old notebooks just to cheer ourself up, we are newly gratified

Three Stars on the Back Stoop

to see how many occasions for thought the world suggests. Often, however, we aren't quite certain just what we meant. For instance, scattered through our now discarded memoranda we find the following cryptic entries:

The army of unalterable bunk.

Prayers for newspaper men.

Nesting season for mares.

Who wrote the line "A rose-red city half as old as time"?

The current fetiches, taboos, and hokums are as hard to expel from the mind as the deboshed melody of some vulgar popular song.

As a child, the phrase "civil engineer" puzzled me—the civility or civics of engineering I could not comprehend.

It's a mistake to conclude that the result of an action was necessarily included in the purpose: i. e.   Effects overlap Causes, e. g. The Tariff.

If every day we are surrounded by astonishment and unexpected adventures in the actual realm, why may it not also be true in the spiritual?

Kipling is the kind of man who, after half a dozen visits to the dentist, would have been able to write a story filled with accurate technical details of dental science.

Sign on Italian restaurant on Park Place: IF YOUR WIFE CAN'T COOK DON'T DIVORCE HER—KEEP HER AS A PET, AND EAT HERE.

Sign on a Manicure Parlour: SPECIAL ATTENTION PAID TO OTHER GIRLS' FELLOWS.

Potboiling—the crackling of a crown of thorns under a pot.

Biography is impossible.   There's no such thing.

Well, the preceding items, lifted more or less at random from one of these notebooks, are sufficient to

The Powder of Sympathy

explain the sense of mystification with which one examines old memoranda. And yet one always hopes that he may chance upon some germ of thought which is worth the fun of expanding it. It reminds us rather of the Janitor Emeritus of the *Post*, an elderly and pensive darkness, who has a fixed idea that some day he is going to find something precious in the various rubbish of the office, and is to be seen gravely poking into baskets and canisters of jetsam in the hope of motion picture magazines, tobacco, and detective stories.

But among these fugitive and sudden scribbles we did find one notation that brings back to us more or less clearly what we had in mind. It was written thus: *People in N. Y. no rooted sense of place.*

We had been thinking of the curious life of those who dwell in city apartments. We are a great lover of apartments every now and then, for a briefly adventurous term; and certainly every one who has read Simeon Strunsky's admirable book *Bellshazzar Court* will have realized how fecund with human episode these great, dense barracks are. But there can be no good life for very long unless one has an opportunity to plant feet on actual soil; to be close witness of earth's colours and seasons; to be able (sovereign pleasure of all) to go out at night and make the circuit of one's terrain and recognize a few stars. There are three stars, for instance, that we see (at certain seasons) from the back stoop when we visit the icebox towards midnight. We suspect them of being the trio known as Orion's Belt. Anyhow, part of our pleasure in life is to notice them occasionally and know that they are

Three Stars on the Back Stoop

still there, or *were* still there when those agile beams
left them to vibrate across all the light-years between
us.

Orion's Belt, by the way, seems to be a Sam Browne,
for it is tilted up diagonally. We will show you ex-
actly what his starry girth looks like, so you can rec-
ognize it:—

*

*

*

The simple and sensuous pleasures of place are not
so easy to enjoy in the city. There is a feeling of un-
reality, of human and mechanical interposition, when
you are snugly nested in a niche of a stone cliff fifteen
stories high. Something stands between you and the
realization of earth. That something may be fine,
comfortable, reassuring, it may be highly stimulant for
the mind; but there is also a loss to the spirit. It is a
loss not to be able to see exactly how Nature tints her
tapestry curtain of gold and bronze, behind which she
quietly shifts the scenes for the next act; and then sud-
denly the curtain is shredded away; the landscape
widens and is transvisible to the eye; going out on the
porch at night you find the trees full not of leaves but
stars.

This is a large topic: we can only hint at it. Science,
criticism, ethics, these are urbane. Poetry and re-
ligion are rustic. Poetry particularly—whether the
writing or the reading of it—thrives best where there is
silence and the foundation on earth. The solid satis-

The Powder of Sympathy

faction of visiting one's own cellar and the brightness of one's own furnace grate, actually set down inside the shell of earth's crust; of knowing one's own chimney shaft open topward to the sky; the fall of autumn acorns rattling on the roof—are sentiments felt rather than understood. But from that quiet fertility of feeling understanding grows gradually. You must be quiet with things before you can love them; and you must love them before you can write about them.

But very likely these fragmentary ideas are true only for those who believe them. It is a way ideas have.

A CHRISTMAS CARD

[*December, 1921*]

AS THE Christmas season approaches, it sits heavily upon our mind that there are some to whom we should like to say a word of respectful admiration. First of these is Woodrow Wilson. This, you may think, is a gesture both irrelevant and impertinent on our part. We cannot help it. We feel, as the Friends say, a "concern." The conjunction of the Christmas month, the Conference on Limitation of Armaments, the hopes and memories of all honest men, Mr. Wilson's coming birthday, makes the occasion irresistible. There are some things that must be said.

The Powder of Sympathy

Woodrow Wilson has found the peace he sought. Never before, perhaps, did a public man enjoy such posthumous privilege in his own lifetime. He has joined (in Melville's noble phrase) "the choice hidden handful of the divine inert." This phrase requires scrutiny. The divinity is not ascribed to Mr. Wilson, but to inertia. Silence, thought, withdrawal from the maddening struggles of mankind—these are divine; these are godlike. If there were ever any doubt as to his having qualities of true greatness, consider the patience and decency of his present silence. It is a silence, one feels, not of bitterness but of honourable dignity.

Sometimes, tucked away in the papers, one finds a single line or so that gives us more to ponder than all the rest of the day's news. Such an item was the following, quoted lately by Mr. Tumulty as having been said by Mr. Wilson to one of his advisers at the Paris Conference:

"M. Clemenceau called me a pro-German and abruptly left the room."

They said this man was impatient and stubborn. Yet he endured insult calmly in the pursuit of his strangely hoped-for peace.

The post-Armistice career of Mr. Wilson has been called a tragedy. We do not see it so. The Paris Conference—it is easy to see it now—was foredoomed to a certain measure of failure. On sand one puts up a tent, not a house. Moreover, in so far as that Conference is concerned, Mr. Wilson has suffered a double

A Christmas Card

fatality. He has never spoken candidly for himself; he has been unfortunate in those who have spoken for him. It has been the habit of those naïf and loyally affectionate souls who have been closest to him to assure us of his subtlety and quicksilver craft. We cannot see it. He has seemed to us, always, a man of genuine simplicity—what would have been called, at one time, a *righteous* man.

It is an odd thing that when you say a character is rooted in simplicity and piety some will conclude that you are sneering. His character is a great character. Those influences which shake and unsettle men's fibre more than anything else it has endured in full measure —adulation and hatred. The anger and mockery which were lavished upon Wilson are interesting to contemplate. But, so far as one can see, they did not trouble that stubborn zeal. There was a Cromwellian grimness and singleness of heart in his battle with Europe. You remember what Cromwell said (if Carlyle can be trusted as a reporter)—

"Would we have Peace without a Worm, lay we Foundations of Justice and Righteousness."

For that he struggled, burdening himself beyond human strength. For that he compromised, as all men do. For that he incurred the malice of all aspirants —both the pure and the impure.

It is amazing to remember the power and depth of that malice. In a perverse way, it is almost encouraging to remember it: it proves so excellently that this

[215]

The Powder of Sympathy

earth is still the fallen star, the cindered Eden, in which merely human failings incur more than human angers. What a gruesome life that of politics must be! And yet when, in our recent history, were more positive virtues and high-minded hopes brought into the muddled ferment of national politics? Do you remember how this man lay at death's door for many silent months, and how ill suppressed were the satisfaction and the sneer? What was his crime? We used to wonder. Only that he had believed the world was ripe for some strokes of simplicity and unselfishness.

Little by little the minds of fair-hearted men are returning to realization and gratitude. There is nothing now accomplished, or even accomplishable, in matters of international dealing, that Woodrow Wilson was not fighting for three years ago. The granolithic minds of the old stand-patters and the luxurious sniffs of young, hot doctrinaires formed for a while a quaint partnership of scorn. Nor would we ourself deny that there were many things to lament. But the world still waits for a competent, understanding, and judicial expression of Woodrow Wilson's service to men. It was not a perfect service, for it was marred by necessary mortal blunders and qualms. For that perhaps we reverence it the more. And when the just tribute comes, perhaps it will come from the hand of some great writer to whom the puerilities of partisan squabble fade into their deserved shadow; to whom the humour and the pathos will be evident; and most evident of all, the dignity and austerity of a great human hope, frustrated and

A Christmas Card

postponed, but an addition to the honour of the race.
Perhaps it will come from the hand of some great
dramatist, with the dramatist's art that can revive
great figures, great moments; can purge the occasion
of what was merely peevish and fortuitous, and remind
us of truths and visions we lost in the hurly-burly of
the time.

It is sheer selfishness on our part to hope that some
such expression may come soon. We are jealous for
the credit of this generation. We are proud to have
lived in days when men suffered so hideously and yet
did and said and wrote great things. We would like
it to be said of this generation that it recognized great-
ness in its own time. That would be an honourable
thing to be able to say. Have we erected, from our
imagination, a figure that is not really there? We
think not. And so, with humility and hesitation, but
impelled by a motive we cannot resist, we would like
to say to Woodrow Wilson that there are many who
gratefully wish him Merry Christmas.

SYMBOLS AND PARADOXES

WE ALWAYS suspected, after reading *The Flying Inn*, that G. K. Chesterton is fond of dogs. And now, reading his book, *The New Jerusalem* (which is full of very gorgeous matter), we learn that at his home in Beaconsfield he is host to both a dog (called "Winkle") and a donkey (called "Trotsky"). Very genial is his picture of the start of his pilgrimage to Palestine and his last farewell to these beasts:

The reader will learn with surprise that my first feeling of fellowship went out to the dog; I am well aware that I lay open my guard to a lunge of wit. . . . He jumped about me, barking like a small battery, under the impression that I was going for a walk; but I could not, alas, take him with me on a stroll to Palestine. . . . The dog's very lawlessness is but an extravagance of loyalty; he will go mad with joy three times on the same day at going out for a walk down the same road. We hear strangely little of the real merits

Symbols and Paradoxes

of animals; and one of them surely is this innocence of
all boredom; perhaps such simplicity is the absence
of sin. I have some sense myself of the sacred duty of
surprise; and the need of seeing the old road as a new
road. But I cannot claim that whenever I go out for
a walk with my family and friends, I rush in front of
them volleying vociferous shouts of happiness; or even
leap up round them attempting to lick their faces. It
is in this power of beginning again with energy upon
familiar and homely things that the dog is really the
eternal type of the Western civilization.

The only thing that bothers us in this: If it had oc-
curred to G. K. C. to prove that the scraper on his
doorstep, or the radish growing in the garden, was the
"eternal type" of Western civilization, would he not
have made out an equally agreeable and convincing
case for it? In fact, only a few steps away from his
home, he came to the crossroads (and well we remember
that crossroads, and the pub thereby—which is it, Mr.
Chesterton: the *Saracen's Head,* or the *Royal White
Hart?*) and there decided that they were the symbol of
civilization which had lost its way. And then, a few
minutes later (in the train, we suppose) the glorious
creature was noticing the heavy clouds that lay over
the landscape, and decided that *they* were the emblem
of our civilization. It takes a good deal of agility to
pursue our pilgrim through this book, for every olive
tree, signboard, sunset, gateway, proves to be a magni-
ficent symbol of some spiritual gorgeousness.

We were sorry that Mr. Chesterton, when leav-
ing Beaconsfield, did not find some symbolism in a
thing which impressed us when we went pilgriming in

The Powder of Sympathy

those parts. Edmund Burke lived there at one time, and we remember reading in some guide-book that his home was "bounded in front by a ha-ha." We thought to ourself at that time, how excellently symbolic it would have been if G. K. C. had bounded his own house in the same way. In fact, we often went along his road to listen for it.

There was another bit of symbolism that used to impress us (it is surprising how quickly one can pick up the habit of symbolizing) when we dallied around Beaconsfield. That was that Edmund Waller is buried under the big walnut tree in the churchyard:

> *Edmundi Waller hic jacet*
> *id quantum morti cessit*

And we thought it pleasant that Mr. Chesterton should have settled in the village sacred to the poet who wrote the loveliest poem ever written on girth—or, rather, on slenderness. You remember, of course, his "On a Girdle."

The average person dearly loves a label—also a libel: and Mr. Chesterton's gnomes—which are sometimes nuggets, sometimes merely nugæ, but always golden—are ticketed as "paradoxes" by those who have small inkling of what a paradox really is. The best definition was that of Don Marquis, our happiest native contemporary practitioner in this art, when he said that if the positive and negative poles of a truth are bent until they meet (or approach) a spark flashes across.

Symbols and Paradoxes

The paradox is the oldest outcry of the philosopher on contemplating the absurdity of the world. Originally a paradox was simply a surprise—a statement contrary to generally accepted opinion, and very likely untrue. As Hamlet said: "This was sometime a paradox, but now the time gives it proof." But latterly we do not grant the virtue of paradox unless the epigram fulfils a double requirement: it must *seem* absurd; it must *be* true, or at any rate true enough to give the mind a sense of cheerful satisfaction. Its essence is that of surprise—which is the essence of humour.

The intellectual growth of humanity is shown by its increasing tolerance of the paradox. The greatest of all Paradoxers was crucified. Every true paradox is a little parable of human fallibility. A parabola is a conic section; a parable, one might say, is a comic section.

Mr. Chesterton once, in a delightful essay called "Christmas," said something that lingers in our mind as an exhibition of the paradox both in its strength and weakness. He wrote:

It is not uncommon nowadays for the insane extremes in reality to meet. Thus I have always felt that brutal Imperialism and Tolstoian nonresistance were not only not opposite, but were the same thing. They are the same contemptible thought that conquest cannot be resisted, looked at from the two standpoints of the conqueror and the conquered. Thus again teetotalism and the really degraded gin-selling and dram-drinking have exactly the same moral philosophy. They are both based on the idea that fermented liquor is not a drink, but a drug.

The Powder of Sympathy

Now a moment's thought will show the reader that while these two paradoxes are equal in wit, they are not equal in truth. The second is gloriously true; the first, delightfully acute as it is, begs the question. For the Tolstoian will retort that he does not maintain that conquest cannot be resisted; but that, on the contrary, it *is* resisted and defeated by passive oppugnance.

The paradox holds the mirror up to nature, but it is not a plane mirror. It dignifies human nature by assuming that the mind is capable of viewing itself in the refraction of absurdity. Thoughtless people speak of the paradox as a reduction to absurdity. That is not so. There are some subjects that have to be elevated to absurdity.

In conclusion: it is a dangerous tool. It must be gingerly handled lest it become—like the pun—a mere verbicide. And towards the fair sex, beware of paradoxes. They esteem but rarely its prankish tooth. Was not Hamlet's downfall—and his betrothed's also— occasioned when he practiced paradoxes on Ophelia?

THE RETURN TO TOWN

IT WAS with somewhat a heavy heart that we pre-
pared to leave Salamis for the winter. Yet inscru-
table lust of adventure spurred us on; the city, also, is
the place for work. In the country one is too comfort-
able, and there are too many distractions. Either
cider, or stars, or the blue sparkle of the furnace fire—
all these require frequent attentions. But it was hard
to part with Long Island's charms in November,
loveliest of months. The copper-coloured woods, the
chrysanthemums, the brisk walk to the morning train,
the yellow crackle of logs in the chimney, the chill dry
whisper of the neighbouring belt of trees heard at mid-
night from an airy veranda—these are some of the ex-
citements we shall miss. Most of all, perhaps, that
stony little unlit lane, traversed in pitch darkness to-
wards supper time, until, coming clear of the trees, you
open up the Dipper, sprawled low across the northern
sky.

It was hard, too, to leave Salamis just when its

The Powder of Sympathy

winter season of innocent gayeties was commencing. You would hardly believe how much is going on! Did you know that that deathless old railroad station is being (as they say of ships) reconditioned? And there's going to be a drug store in Salamis Heights. The new Methodist church is nearly finished—and, most glamorous of all, we now have an actual tea-room at the entrance to the Salamis Estates. When you are motoring out that way you can see if we don't speak the truth. In another five years, most likely, we shall have street lights along our lonely wood road to Green Escape—and pavements—and gas to cook with. But there never will be quite as many fairies in the woods as there have been these past three years.

But, perhaps fortunately, the day set for moving into town was wet and drizzly. And the labour of piling into Dame Quickly various baggages, hampers, toys, a go-cart, and the component railings, girders, rods, springs and mattresses of two cribs was lively enough to oust from the mind any pangs of mere sentiment. The mind of one who has accomplished that task, in shirt-sleeves under a dripping weather, is heated enough to make him ready for any sort of adventurous foray. The Dame, also, grossly overloaded, and travelling smartly on greasy ways, was skiddish. As is ever our fortune, we found the road through Astoria torn up for repairs. This involved a circuit along a most horrible bypath, where our ill-adjusted freight leaped crazily with every lurch, go-cart and mattresses descended on our neck, and the violence of the bumping caused the crib-girders to burst through the rear of the Dame's

The Return to Town

canopy. Also we incurred, and probably deserved, a stern rebuke from a gigantic policeman on Second Avenue. To tell the truth, in a downshoot of rain and peering desperately through a streaming wind-shield, we did not know he was a policeman at first. We thought he was an L pillar.

Yet, when both voyages were safely accomplished—one for the baggage, and one for the household: it would be harder to say which lading was the tighter squeeze—what an exhilaration to move once more in the city of our adoring. It is true that we began by making an immediate enemy in the apartment house, for, as we were quite innocently taking a trunk upstairs in the elevator, assisted by the cheerful elderly attendant, a lady living in the same house entered by chance and burst into violent reproach because *her* baggage had had to go aloft in the freight elevator. She accused the attendant of favouritism; to which he, quite placidly, explained that this particular baggage had been delivered at the front door in a private car. This compliment to the Dame pleased us, but knowing nothing of the rules, and being wet and pensive, we pretended to be an expressman and said naught. The only other shock was when we took the Dame to a neighbouring garage to recuperate for a few days. (We were glad, then, it had been raining, for the well-loved vehicle looked very sleek and shiny, and it was too dark for the garage man to notice the holes in her top. We wouldn't want him to sneer at her, and his garage, we observed, was full of very handsome cars.) When he said it would cost the Dame $1.50 a night to

The Powder of Sympathy

live there we were a little horrified. That, we reflected, was what we used to pay ourself at the old Continental Hotel in Philly, the inn where the Prince of Wales (the old one) and Dickens and Lincoln and others stayed. We now look with greater and greater astonishment at all the cars we see in New York. How can any one afford to keep them?

We were dispatched to do some hasty marketing, in time for supper. We made off to our favourite shopping street—Amsterdam Avenue. Delightedly we gazed into those alluring windows. In a dairy, a young lady of dark and appealing loveliness made us welcome. When we ordered milk and laid in a stock of groceries, making it plain to her (by consulting a list) that we were speaking on behalf of the head of the house, she urged us to advise Titania to open an account. Money she seemed loath to accept: it could all be paid for at the end of the month, she said. It is well to shop referring perplexedly to a little list. This proves that you are an humble, honest paterfamilias, acting only under orders. To such credit is always lavish, and fair milkmaids generously tender.

Various tradesmen in that neighbourhood were surprised, in the tail end of a wet and depressing day, by unexpected increments of traffic. "Just nick the bone?" inquired the butcher, when, from our list, we read him the item about rib lamb chops. "Yes, just nick the bone," we assented, not being very definite on the subject. We were interested in admiring the thick sawdust on the floor, very pleasant to slide the foot upon. The laundryman was just closing when we ar-

The Return to Town

rived with our bundle. "Here's a new customer for
you," we announced. Whatever private sorrows he
has were erased from his manly forehead. He told us
that he also does tailoring. Cleaning and pressing, he
insisted. We had a private feeling, a little shameful,
that he hasn't got as good a customer as he imagines.
Next door to the tailor, by the way, and right opposite
the apartment house, is a carpenter who advertises his
skill at bookshelves.

How different it is from Salamis nights. Hanging
out of the kitchen window (having gone to the rear of
the apartment to see what the icebox is like: it's a
beauty)—instead of Orion's Belt and the dry rustle of
the trees, we see those steep walls of lighted windows,
discreetly blinded, hear sudden shrills of music from
above and below. Just through the wall, as we lie
abed, we can hear the queer droning whine of the ele-
vator; through the open window, the clang of trolleys
on Broadway. Hunting through the books that belong
in the furnished apartment, after startling ourself by
reading Mr. D. H. Lawrence's poems called *Look! We
Have Come Through!* we found an old Conan Doyle—
always our favourite bedtime author. *The Adventures
of Gerard*, indeed, and we are going to have a go at it
immediately.

Yes, it's very different from Salamis; but Adventure
is everywhere, and we like to take things as we find
them. We have never been anywhere yet, whether in
the steerage of the *Mauretania* or in a private lunch-
room at the Bankers' Club, where there wasn't more
amusement than we deserved.

[227]

MAXIMS AND MINIMS

KINSPRITS

You know how it is: there are books that magi-
cally convey a secret subtle intimation that *you* are
the only reader who has ever, will ever, wholly grasp
their elusive wit and charm. So it is with certain
people. I think of my friend Pausanias. He is quiet,
shy; he makes his points so demurely, so quaintly,
that you sometimes think, sadly, of all the occult little
japes he may be making in the weeks that elapse when
you don't see him . . . and no one, perhaps,
"gets" them. Folly, of course—and yet I have seen
his eye widen and brighten as it caught mine across the
dinner table, and I knew that he and I, secretly, had
both caught some faint, delicious savour of absurdity
and human queerness—something that no one else

Maxims and Minims

there (I strongly believed it) had quite so sharply tasted. Yes, you can catch his eye—no word is necessary. Just a slow, enjoying, gentle grin. Across the great clamour of blurb and bunk, across the huge muddle of beauty, weariness, and frustration that makes up our daily life—I am always catching his eye.

* * * * * * *

JOURNALISM AND LITERATURE

Art is the only human power that can make life stand still. Each of us, desperately clutching his identity amid the impalpable onward pour of Time and Thought, finds only in art—and chiefly in written art—a means to halt that ceaseless cruel drift. Literature was invented to halt life, to hold it still for us to examine and admire.

Here you may see the essential distinction between literature and journalism. For journalism was devised to hurry life on even faster, to give the already whirling wheel an insane accelerating fillip. Journalism is, actually, a pastime; literature, a stoptime. I refer, of course, not to the journalism of facts, which is a department of government rather than of letters; but to the journalism of fancy. In great books life (however troubled and violent in itself) stands pure and unvexed, unfretted by time and interruption.

There are many schools of journalism; for journalism, being only a hasty knack, can readily be taught. There are no schools of literature, for that is born in your own hearts only, and by manifold joys and disgusts. If it

[229]

is in you, you shall know; the disease will grow more and more potent. If it is in you, you shall be dedicated to misery unguessed by the easy minds beside you. A great poet spoke of hovering between two worlds, one dead, one powerless to be born. That shall be your mental lot. You shall realize, more and more, that the bustling cheery life of the general is, in some seizures, dead to your spirit: and yet that new brave world of imagination, which travails in your heart, can never quite come to paper. Would you know the mood and emotion that move behind literature, read Arnold's *Scholar Gipsy*. I love journalism and honour it; but it must be added that it inhabits a different world from literature, and does not even faintly understand the language that literature speaks.

*   *   *   *   *   *   *

HOBBES

There are some famous books which are the delight of scholars but hardly at all known to the amateur reader. Of such, we think of Thomas Hobbes' *Leviathan*. It is so nobly sagacious and entertaining that with a little trouble spent on rephrasing his stuff and giving it snappy captions we could probably sell it to a long chain of newspapers and enter into competition with the Syndicated Spinozas who prey upon the public appetite for aphorisms.

Hobbes' wisdom is of the shrewd and nipping sort. If we had to choose but one passage, to show a seventeenth-century mind at its best, we should pluck his

Maxims and Minims

remarks on Laughter—famous indeed, but probably
little known to casual readers. See the clear stream of
the mind flowing in a channel of granite prose:—

Sudden glory is the passion which maketh those
grimaces called laughter; and is caused either by some
sudden act of their own that pleaseth them, or by the
apprehension of some deformed thing in another by
comparison whereof they suddenly applaud themselves.
And it is incident most to them that are conscious of the
fewest abilities in themselves: who are forced to keep
themselves in their own favour by observing the im-
perfections of other men.   And therefore much laughter
at the defects of others is a sign of pusillanimity.   For
of great minds one of the proper works is to help and
free others from scorn, and compare themselves only
with the most able.

On the contrary, sudden dejection is the passion that
causeth weeping, and is caused by such accidents as
suddenly take away some vehement hope or some prop
of their power; and they are most subject to it that
rely principally on helps external, such as are women
and children.   Therefore some weep for the loss of
friends, others for their unkindness, others for the
sudden stop made to their thoughts of revenge by recon-
ciliation.   But in all cases, both laughter and weeping
are sudden motions, custom taking them both away.
For no man laughs at old jests, or weeps for an old
calamity.

The vain-glory which consisteth in the feigning or
supposing of abilities in ourselves which we know are
not is most incident to young men, and nourished by
the histories or fictions of gallant persons, and is cor-
rected oftentimes by age and employment.

*   *   *   *   *   *   *

The Powder of Sympathy

There is a certain department store on the slope of Murray Hill which has in it a gallery much frequented by ladies for meeting their friends. Once in a while we have an appointment there to wait for Titania, and always we find it an entertaining corner of the world. Along one side of the gallery is a long line of telephone booths, and we know nothing more amusing than to stroll past the glass doors, with apparently abstracted and meditative air, to watch the faces of the fair captives within. How admirable a contrivance is the feminine face for reflecting the emotions! Some you will see talking animatedly, with bright colour, sparkling eyes, every appearance of mirth and merry cheer. Others are waiting, all anguish and grievance, for some dilatory connection; their small brows heavy with perplexity. Often it seems to be necessary, for some mysterious sharing of secrets or shopping plans, for two ladies to occupy the same booth at a time; how they do it we cannot guess; but they sit demurely squeezed upon one another and their faces appear side by side, both apparently talking at once into the receiver. Through the glass pane this offers a curious sight, apparently a lady with two heads; muffled by the barrier, shrill squeaks and conjectures are dimly heard. There are ladies, generous of physique, who find it hard enough to press in singly; when they seek to arise they are held tightly by the cage and a great wrench and backing outward are necessary. Particularly on a Saturday, shortly before matinée time, are these lively

[232]

creatures full of animation and derring-do. A gay and vivid panorama of human frailty, only surpassed in quaint absurdity by a similar row of men in the phone booths of a large cigar store.

* * * * * * *

OF STREET CLEANING

(*By Our Own Lord Bacon*)

Snow is a deposit fair in itself, but a shrewd thing in a city. Where ways be crowded and traffic insisteth, let there be alacrity and stirring on the part of the city servants, lest the public have occasion of murmuring. Of streets which need purifying, there be three kinds: as Broadway, which is treacle; Fifth Avenue, syrup; and uptown, which is soup and all manner of beastliness. So also of snow there be three sorts, the dry and powdery; the wet and slushy, liquefying soon; the granular and sleety, whereof the latter adhereth long and occasioneth sudden prostrations, unwholesome to human dignity but opportunity of sport to the vulgar. When men are checked in their desires to pass to and fro without let or stoppage, then must the prince be wary to reason with the commuters, who being ever great self-lovers, *sui amantes sine rivali*, are like to be disproportionate in outcry. And for the most part, the subway will be still current, but small praise accrueth thereto from citizens, sudden cattle in protest but tardy to acknowledge favour. This is not handsome. Of the surface cars I will not speak; let them be, for the occasion, as though they existed not. For though there

[233]

be some talk about revival of the service when the Broadway slot be picked and scalded by hand, yet is this but vaunting and idle boast. There is no impediment in the streets but may be wrought out by resolute labour. Of block parties, flame throwers, tractors, steam-ploughs and other ingenuities, I like them not. These be but toys. Let men toil with wit and will, by pick and shovel and horse-cart. This is best for the public.

*   *   *   *   *   *   *

DR. OSLER

"In seventy or eighty years" (said Thomas Browne, M. D.) "a man may have a deep Gust of the World, know what it is, what it can afford, and what 'tis to have been a Man. Such a latitude of years may hold a considerable corner in the general Map of Time."

Surely no modern thinker has taken a deeper gust of life or pondered more charitably over the difficult problems of the race than Sir William Osler, a true follower and kinsprit of the wise physician of Norwich. "The Old Humanities and the New Science," his last public address (given in Oxford, May 16, 1919), was the capsheaf of that long series of writings and speakings in which Dr. Osler unlocked his generous, humane heart and gave inspiring counsel to his fellows.

It was an occasion that even the most severe brevity must describe as of happy import. Osler, a physician and a man of science, had been honoured by the presidency of the Classical Association, Great Britain's most distinguished gathering of the men who have made the

Maxims and Minims

culture of the antique world their touchstone in life.
And Dr. Osler, himself a keen classical student, did not
permit himself merely gracious and suave messages.
Pleading for a new bridal of science and the classics,
in that delightful and urbane chaff which he knew
so well to administer, he pointed out the barrenness of
the tradition that has made the famous "More Humane
Letters" of Oxford entirely neglect the workings and
winnings of the science that has transformed the world.
Dr. Osler, in his great career, perhaps never spoke with
more convincing persuasion than when he pointed out
that even in their own province of the classical tongues
the modern humanists have passed over the scientific
work of the ancients, as for instance in Aristotle and
Lucretius.

Among men who err and are baffled, but still blunder
eagerly and hopefully in the magnificent richness of the
natural world, there arise ever and again such figures as
Osler's, a pride and a consolation to their comrades.
Men, alas! are slow in finding the treasures that lie close
about them. Dr. Osler's essays are too little known
among general readers. His all-embracing humanity,
his mind packed with wisdom and beauty, his humour
and his sagacious and persistent method in the conduct
of a crowded life, make him a figure exceptionally help-
ful to contemplate. This last of his essays needs to be
read not only by all educators, but by all who have any
rational ideals of life, and who need, every now and
then, to surmount the troubled stream of quotidian
affairs and focus their visions more clearly.

No sensible man doubts that, if haste and confusion

[235]

The Powder of Sympathy

and greed do not overcome us, the world should stand to-day on the sill of a new Renaissance, a new empire of the mind, in which the old foolish antagonism of science and the so-called "humanities" will be only a vain and dusty rumour. What are "liberal" studies, one may ask? Why, surely, studies that *liberate*—that set the spirit free from the oppression of sordid and small motives, that stir and urge it toward generous achievement and the assistance of misfortune. When did letters arrogate to themselves the heavenly adjective *belles?* Are there not the *belles sciences* also? And is the biplane now soaring over the olive-shining Hudson any less lovely than the most precious sonnet ever anchored and flattened in persisting ink?

This essay of Dr. Osler's shows one the pulse and heartbeat of modern science, the tender spirit of idealism that urges so much of the technical investigation of our time. In Dr. Osler, as in hundreds of other scientists less known and perhaps less gifted in public utterance, there is the union of the two Hippocratic ideals which the great Canadian physician laid before himself as his guides in life—the union of *philanthropia* and *philotechnia*—a love of humanity joined to a love of his craft.

To infect the average man with the spirit of the humanities, Dr. Osler said, is the highest aim of education. And this brilliant address of his is a crowning instance of the way in which, in his mind, the practical service of science was beautified by the liberal and imperishable spirit of classical thought.

* * * * * * *

Maxims and Minims

We have just been reading what we honestly believe is the most fascinating book in the world. It is, we must confess, very much in the vein of this modern realism, because it is written in a terse, staccato, and even abrupt style, although always well balanced. The general effect, we admit, is depressing, though that may be only our own personal reaction, because the plot is one with which we are intimately familiar. Every now and then the action rises to a climax when we think it is going to end happily after all; but then something always occurs to sadden us. Occasionally it gives us moments of gruesome suspense, followed by flashes of temporary optimism. The general technique is distinctly that of the grieving Russian prose writers, for the total effect is gloomy and grim. The critics have had nothing to say about this book, but for us it has cumulating interest.

We find we forgot to mention the title of the above volume, which is issued in very handy format, bound in limp brown leather. We mean, of course, our bank book.

*   *   *   *   *   *   *

We have been looking over the catalogue of Coventry Patmore's library, issued by Everard Meynell at "The Serendipity Shop," London. The following note interested us; some of our vigorous readers, now that the

The Powder of Sympathy

wooing season is toward, may find in it a gentle technical hint:

Patmore told Dr. Garnett that during his courtship, wishing to be sure that a congeniality of taste existed between himself and Emily Andrews, he lent her Emerson's Essays, asking her to mark the passages that most struck her, and on getting the book back was delighted to find that the marks were those which he would have made for himself.

According to Mr. Meynell's catalogue, the copy of Emerson referred to is inscribed, in Patmore's hand: "Emily Andrews, June 24, 1847." Emerson's efficacy in the rôle of Cupid may be judged from the fact that the two were married September 11, 1847.

One wonders if Patmore applied the same test before his two subsequent marriages (1864, 1881).

* * * * * * *

ADVICE TO YOUNG WRITERS

A gentleman asks us to give some advice to young men intending to enter journalism. Well, we would say, get a job as a sporting writer. That is where the real fun lies. Being a sporting writer is hot stuff; it keeps you out in the open air, you are respected and even admired by the least easily impressionable classes, such as policemen, car conductors, and office boys; you have immense fun inventing new ways of saying things (which is the groundwork of good literature), get a great many free meals, have your expenses paid, meet people who have high-powered cars and put them at your disposal, and your lightest word is deemed important enough to be put on a telegraph wire and flashed to the office for an EXTRA. If you write about such minor matters as war and peace, poetry, books, or the beauty of this, that, and the other, you will be hidden demurely away on an inside page and there is no particular hurry about it.

The other day at the Polo Grounds we noticed a hard-boiled fan leaving the stand after the game. As he passed out onto the field he suddenly saw the gang of reporters finishing up their stories and the instruments clattering beside them. "Gee," he cried, "look at all the writers!" And with a real awe he turned to his companion and said: "Their stuff goes all over the world."

We contend that Joseph Conrad, Thomas Hardy, James Branch Cabell, Joe Hergesheimer, Bernard Shaw, Rudyard Kipling, and Lord Dunsany, sitting side by side on a bench writing short stories for a wager, would not have elicited such a gust of reverent admiration from our friend.

We are not joking. You can have more fun, and get better paid for it, as a sporting reporter than in any other newspaper job. And there is in it a bigger opportunity for men of real originality.

* * * * * * *

A GREAT REPORTER

We have been reading—for the first time, we blush to admit—the *Journal of a Tour to the Hebrides*, in the magnificent ten-volume edition of Boswell published by Gabriel Wells. It is the ideal book for

The Powder of Sympathy

reading on the train, and causes us to reassert that Jamie was one of the world's greatest reporters. If we were running a newspaper we would give a copy of this book to every man on the news staff. Professor Tinker in his introduction calls it "perhaps the sprightliest book of travels in the language." Indeed, this is Boswell *in excelsis*, and it warms us to note the magnificent zest and gusto and triumphant happiness that peep between all his paragraphs. Happy, happy man, he had his adored Doctor to himself; he had him, at last, actually in Scotland; they were on holiday together! "Master of the Hebridean Revels," Tinker charmingly calls him. What an immortal touch is this, of the somewhat baffled Mrs. Boswell, who must have thought the expedition a perverse absurdity. This is on the day Johnson and Boswell left Edinburgh—

She did not seem quite easy when we left her; but away we went!

Perfect, perfect—even down to the exclamation point. We have not got very far in the Tour—only some fifty pages—but we are drowned deep in the engulfing humour and fecund humanity of the book. What an appetite for life, what a glorious naïf curiosity! What a columnist Boswell would have made! He quotes Johnson to this effect—

I love anecdotes. I fancy mankind may come, in time, to write all aphoristically, except in narrative; grow weary of preparation, and connection, and illustration, and all those arts by which a big book is made.

Maxims and Minims

Boswell, with superb dramatic instinct, unconsciously adopted the most triumphant subtlety of manœuvre. He put himself in the posture of a boob in order to draw out the characteristic good things of the great men he admired. He fished passionately for human oddity, and used any bait at all that was to hand—even himself. To see the two together on Boswell's artfully contrived stage—Scotland, which he knew would elicit the Doctor's most genuine humours, prejudices, shrewd manly observations—and in the bright light of a junketing adventure—ah, here is a bellyful of art. What a pair: the subtle simpleton, the simple-minded sage!

*   *   *   *   *   *   *

AN UNFAIR ADVANTAGE

Of course, it's the oldest spoof in the world; and also it isn't quite fair; but we felt that (for private reasons) we owed it to ourself to chaff a certain publisher friend. So we diligently typed out the first dozen or so of Shakespeare's sonnets, and, making use of a borrowed name and address kindly lent us by a colleague, submitted them to the publisher.

We accompanied them by a pseudonymous letter which we truly think was something of a work of art, it was so amiably true to the sort of thing that publishers are accustomed to receive. We explained that these were the first of a series of 154 sonnets, and added that though many of our friends thought them good, we feared their affectionate partiality. We were submitting only a few, we said, in the hope of frank criti-

cism from a great publishing house. If we were lucky
enough to have them accepted the rest would be forth-
coming; and the volume (we hoped) would be bound in
red leather with very wide margins and a blank page
at the front for autographing. And a good deal more
innocent and hopeful meditation.

We had to wait some time for the reply—and had
even begun to fear that the publisher had spotted our
jape. But no—here is the answer that came:

We are sorry that after a careful consideration of
your "Sonnets" we cannot make a proposal for publi-
cation. We fear that we are lacking in a real enough
enthusiasm to push the book as it must be pushed to
bring about any success.

We regret, too, that we cannot comply with your
request to criticise the work, but it is against our policy
to offer criticism on material which we cannot accept
for publication. We handle so many manuscripts that
we could not do the work justice, and then, too, we are
diffident about offering suggestions when you may find
a publisher who will like your work just as it stands. In
general, however, we may say that, so far as we can
judge, we thought that the work was not up to standard.

Thank you for giving us the opportunity of consider-
ing your manuscript. It is being returned to you by
mail.

We now lay this before a candid world and ask our
friend how much blackmail we can get out of him to
refrain from publishing his identity?

Yet we admit it wasn't quite fair. A knowledge of
Shakespeare's Sonnets is no necessary equipment for

[242]

Maxims and Minims

successful publishing. And some of them, if you are taken unawares, do sound a bit preposterous.

*   *   *   *   *   *   *

CARAWAY SEEDS

It seemed to us that we saw a deep significance in the fact, told by Lytton Strachey in his *Queen Victoria*, that the Queen's pious governess, Lehzen, was a fanatic about caraway seeds. Mr. Strachey says:

Her passion for caraway seeds, for instance, was uncontrollable. Little bags of them came over to her from Hanover, and she sprinkled them on her bread and butter, her cabbage, and even her roast beef.

Surely throughout the whole Victorian era ¦the attentive observer can discern the faint but pungent musk of the mild, bland, uncandid caraway. We ourself, in our early youth, crossed the trail of that seed more than once, in small cakes and patties, and instinctively revolted from it. If there is any emblem symbolic of the Victorian age, perhaps it is the caraway seed, a thing that Greenwich Village, we dare say, has never encountered even in its most enterprising tearoom. The kingdom of Victoria, we suggest, was like a grain of caraway seed; but it became a tree so vast that the fowls of the air lodged in the branches thereof.

*   *   *   *   *   *   *

BLUNT'S DIARIES

We have a fear that the two volumes of Wilfrid Scawen Blunt's Diaries—published here last year by Alfred Knopf—are not as widely known as they should

The Powder of Sympathy

be. This is natural, for the two big volumes are expensive, but they are a mine of most interesting material. They are a liberal education in the truth *quot homines tot sententiæ*—in other words, that there are infinite matters of difference among honourable men.

Blunt was a gallant dissenter and whole-hearted skeptic about civilization. Of course these aristocratic rebels, who have never had to pass through the gruelling discipline of middle-class life; who have always been free to travel, to ramble about to witty week-end parties at country houses, ride blooded horses, sit up all night drinking port wine and talking brilliantly with Cabinet Ministers, have (or so it seems to us) a fairly easy time compared to the humdrum plod who wambles through a stiff continuous stint of hard work and still keeps a bit of rebellion in his heart. And of course, since Blunt condemned almost everything in European politics throughout his lifetime, one begins to suspect that he was almost too pernickety. Of the unnumbered British statesmen whom he roasted, not *all* can have been either fools or knaves. The law of average forbids. But a protestant of that sort is a magnificently healthy and useful person to have about. He had a habit of assuming that Egypt, India, Ireland, Turkey, Germany, were always right, and England necessarily wrong. When a country has a number of citizens like that and regards them affectionately, it is a sign that it is beginning to grow up. One of Blunt's remarks to Margot Asquith is worth remembering: "There is nothing so demoralizing for a country as to put people in prison for their opinions."

Maxims and Minims

But the casual reader ought to have a go at Blunt's Diaries because they are a rich deposit of pithy human anecdote. We see him, at the age of sixty-six or thereabouts, attending a performance of Hippolytus, translated by Murray. "At the end of it we were all moved to tears, and I got up and did what I never did before in a theatre, shouted for the author, whether for Euripides or Gilbert Murray I hardly knew." With Coquelin père he goes to have lunch with Margot Asquith. Her little daughter, twelve years old (now, of course, Princess Bibesco, whose short stories are well worth your reading), dressed in a Velasquez costume, was called on to recite poems. "Coquelin good-naturedly suggested that 'perhaps Mademoiselle would be shy,' but Margot would not hear of it. 'There is no shyness,' she said, 'in this family.'" Any lover of the human comedy will find intense joy in Blunt's comments on Edward VII, for instance. When his antipathies were aroused, Blunt lived up to his name. Roosevelt's speech in Cairo in 1910 praising British rule in Egypt was a red rag to the elderly skeptic, who considered that Britain had no business anywhere on earth outside her own island. His comment in his journal was: "He is a buffoon of the lowest American type, and roused the fury of young Egypt to the boiling point . . . he is now at Paris airing his fooleries, and is to go to Berlin, a kind of mad dog roaming the world." It is quaint that the humanitarians and intense lovers of their kind are always the most brutal in attack upon those with whom they disagree.

The Powder of Sympathy

There are also innumerable snapshots of men of letters in mufti. Rossetti, for instance, throwing a cup of tea at Meredith's face. Most of Meredith, Blunt found unreadable. His picture of Francis Thompson's last days is unforgettable. For our own part we find particular amusement in the little sideviews of Hilaire Belloc—a neighbour in Sussex in the later years. It is disconcerting to learn that Belloc's horse "Monster," of whom the hilarious Hilaire speaks so highly in a number of essays, is "a very ancient mare which he rides in blinkers. He is no great horseman." Belloc coming to picnic with a bottle of wine in his pocket; Belloc out-talking Alfred Austin, Arthur Balfour, and indeed everyone else; Belloc wondering if he would be given a peerage; Belloc groaning because he has sworn off liquor during Lent, and Belloc delightfully and extremely wrong in the days just preceding the war—insisting that Germany was unprepared and afraid of France—these are the sort of things that cannot by any stretch of exaggeration be called malicious tattle; they are the genial byplay of civilization that keeps us reminded that those we love and admire may be not less absurd than ourselves.

There is much real beauty in the book, too. Blunt was a poet of very considerable charm, and a little story told by a former schoolmate of his seems rather characteristic. When a child he used to keep caterpillars in paper boxes; but he always pricked holes in the lids in the form of the constellations—so that the imprisoned caterpillars might think they were still out of doors and could see the stars.

Maxims and Minims

It's a queer thing. Those caterpillars, somehow or other, make us think of newspaper men.

*   *   *   *   *   *   *

GENIUS

Occasionally we have fired off a culverin or two in honour of Stella Benson, that remarkably agile and humorous creature, who is, with May Sinclair and "Elizabeth," one of our favourite female novelists. So we are particularly pleased to have F. H. P. recall to us a passage about the Dog David, in *Living Alone:*

David Blessing Brown, a dog of independent yet loving habit, had spent about four-fifths of his life in the Brown family. He was three years old and though ineligible for military service made a point of wearing khaki about his face and in a symmetrical heart-shaped spot near his tail. To Sarah Brown he was the Question and the Answer, his presence was a constant playtime for her mind; so well was he loved that he seemed to her to move in a little mist and glamour of love.   .   .   .

I believe that Sarah Brown had loved the Dog David so much that she had given him a soul. Certainly other dogs did not care for him. David said that they had found out that his second name was Blessing and that they laughed at him for it. His face was seamed with the scars of their laughing. But I know that the enmity had a more fundamental reason than that. I know that when men speak with the tongues of angels they are shunned and hated by men, and so I think that when dogs approach humanity too nearly they are banished from the love of their own kind.

The Powder of Sympathy

If you do not recognize, even in that little random passage, the curious quality of Stella Benson's talent, then we fear (brave friends) we can never agree about literature. In her writing we always seem to see that special and bewildering richness that we prize most of all; something that does not lie in any particular nicety or adornment of words, but in an underrunning flavour and queer subtlety of meaning. Is there any subject in the world more trite, more shopworn, and defaced by acres of blab than Dogs and their relations to mankind? There is not. And yet see how Stella Benson, without one pompous or pretentious word, and with a humour both mocking and tender, has not only said something new, but something which, as soon as it is said, becomes old, because it is permanent. That is what, in lieu of a better word, we are inclined to call genius, and we have never read a page of Miss Benson's work which did not show it.

*   *   *   *   *   *   *

EMBARRASSMENTS

Among our numerous embarrassments we don't know any more painful than being compelled, the other day, to expose our theory of rolltop housekeeping to an insurance man. Old Henry Sonneborn, Jr., of Philadelphia (who is, let us explain, the only insurance man with whom we ever do business) came over to arrange some alterations in our complicated scheme of "protection." But he caught us unawares, and when he wanted to see some of our receipts we had to go hunting through our desk while he was sitting right there watching us.

Maxims and Minims

We explained our theory. Now, Henry, we said, there are only three places where that missing receipt can possibly be. It may be in one of the pigeonholes that run due east of the foc's'le of the desk. If it isn't there, it will be in the right-hand front corner of the principal drawer, where we put things while waiting for a chance to file them. If it isn't there, it will be in the tin tobacco box that we keep hidden under the unanswered letters. We feared that Henry would think us very unbusinesslike, but he was polite and kind, as always.

We went through the drawer first. Henry was a bit disconcerted to find it so dusty; and so were we. We found a clay pipe that we hadn't seen for a long time; we found some foreign stamps that we have been saving to send to a small boy in Philadelphia. We tried with these to distract Henry's attention from the object of search. We asked him if his little boy was a stamp collector. But Henry kept bringing us back to the receipt, which was necessary for some reason. He said he needed that receipt to complete some scheme he had for reducing our overhead; the best authorities on finance, he said, are agreed that no man has any *right* to attempt to save money before he is 40; no, he should put it into insurance. We tried to keep Henry talking while we were scuffling about through the back of the desk. We thought that perhaps the receipt would turn up unexpectedly; we didn't want him to notice that we were looking in parts of the desk where we had explained it could not possibly be.

Damnation, Henry, we said; it isn't our fault that

The Powder of Sympathy

this desk is in such a mess; we have the most orderly instincts, but our clients keep dumping stuff on us so fast that we can't ever catch up with it.

It was a queer coincidence, we thought, that when we went out to lunch that day we noticed at 56 Wall Street a tablet in honour of Morris Robinson, who "established on this spot the business of modern life insurance." He was a Canadian, the tablet says. We're glad he wasn't an American.

In the meantime we are going to have another look through those pigeonholes.

*   *   *   *   *   *   *

AN IDEA

We do not often spend time thinking up ways of surprising humanity with kindness; yet when we stand in line at the bank while a queue of merry merchants ahead of us are drawing out huge payroll sums which take about five minutes each to be counted and recounted, a blithe thought comes our way. It is this: On some Saturday morning, when banking traffic is particularly heavy, we will gather half a dozen friends of ours who have nothing to do. We will go round to the bank and stand in line, all seven of us. As we draw nearer and nearer to the window we will watch the anguished faces of those behind, despairingly counting the number of people that still stand between them and the cherished teller. Then just as the first of our seven gets up to the window we will all slip deftly away and enjoy ourselves by watching the joyous elation of the man who thought himself eighth in line and now finds himself

[250]

Maxims and Minims

next to the grill. All down the impatient throng passes
a tremor of surprised pleasure. Then we will move on
to the next bank and do the same thing.

* * * * * * *

ALGEBRA FOR URCHINS

We wish we weren't so rusty in our mathematics.
One of our favourite projects has always been to write
an algebra book for the use of the Urchin when he gets
a little older. This algebra would be in the form of a
story in which the problems would be introduced natu-
rally into the movement of the tale, and each one would
be (if we could persuade him to do it) illustrated by
Fontaine Fox.

The problems, moreover, would deal with facts and
topics familiar to the Urchin. One problem, for in-
stance, would run something as follows:

Riding in Dame Quickly along the North Hempstead
turnpike, the Urchin notices that a man is walking on
the sidewalk but at just such a pace that a telephone
pole prevents him from being recognized. Attempting
to see who the pedestrian is, and foiled by the fact that
the simultaneous motions of Dame Quickly and the
man on the sidewalk keep the pole constantly in the
line of sight, the Urchin becomes interested in the prob-
lem. He notes that the speedometer indicates 22 miles
an hour. He persuades his father to stop the car and
measure the width of the road and the sidewalk. Dame
Quickly stops opposite the pole and the measurements
are taken. It is 24 feet from the Dame to the pole.
The line along which the man was walking, down the

[251]

The Powder of Sympathy

middle of the sidewalk, was three feet from the pole.
How fast was the man walking?*

*　　*　　*　　*　　*　　*　　*

A MODEST SCAFFOLD FOR PHILOSOPHERS

We have been meditating on the dissimilar conduct
of cats and dogs, since we added a kitten (named
Pepys) to our household roster.

The dog, plainly, is a boob, for he tries so hard to
please and ingratiate the Masters of the Event, his
deities.　Whereas the cat, while calmly recognizing the
paramountcy of the gods, goes ahead in every way
within his power to circumvent and outwit their con-
trol.　The dog, poor honest simpleton, shows his gen-
uine and unselfish affection for his deities; the cat
never makes up to them unless he wants something
from them, or feels that a little friendly caressing
would be agreeable.　The cat is 100 per cent. pro-feline.
The dog, we reckon, is at least 30 per cent. pro-human.
You open the back door.　If the cat wants to go
abroad, he will streak through without an instant's
hesitation; but the dog will wait, politely, until he is
sure whether you wish him to go out.　Question, then,
for philosophic ruminators—Do not the domestic gods
secretly respect the cat a little more because they know
he is inwardly hostile and contemptuous and a perfect
ego?　A whole rationale of heaven and hell may be
quizzed out of this matter.

*　　*　　*　　*　　*　　*　　*

---

*The answer, if you care to work it out, seems to be 2¾ miles per
hour.

Maxims and Minims

We have been considerably humiliated lately by the fact that although we once studied French with some persistence, and enjoy nothing more than reading such demi-gods as the chrysostom Bourget (a celestial ironist far too little known in this country)—humiliated, we repeat, that our spoken French is so appalling. Lately, as the surprising result of an advt. in the *Herald*, Titania landed an elderly female French cook who speaks no word of English. And if you speak French no better than we do, figure to yourself the complexities of trying to explain to Celeste the workings of a kerosene water-heater (we have no gas in the rustic Salamis Estates) while Titania (whose French is better than ours) stands by squeaking with cruel mirth. Comme ça:

Voyez vous, Celeste, l'huile—comment dit-on en français le liquide?—le petrole? Ah, oui—eh bien, le petrole entre par là, dans le petit cylindre, vous prenez moi, hein?—et donc on place le cylindre comme ça— mais pas comme ça, comprenez?—et donc le petrole marche (quand le—comment appelle-t-on le *wick?* le petit toile ici—le mèche? ah oui!—quand le mèche est en ordre laborieux—telle quelle ce n'est pas maintenant)—*ye gods, Titania, give me a hand with this explanation*—le petrole marche en haut—mais voyez vous, ceci n'est pas un mèche honnete-à-dieu; c'est d'asbeste; on place le soi-disant mèche—(le *burner* on dit en anglais) comme ainsi ici bas, et donc on allume une allumette et vous directez le feu par ici, par là, et après le feu s'eteint vous reallumez avec patience. Du patience,

[253]

The Powder of Sympathy

toujours, avec ces poêles à l'huile,—et prenez garde,
ne replacez pas ces cylindres à flamme auparavant
que le feu a monté, et exhibite quelque vitalité, vous
voyez?

Eh bien; en une heure peut-etre vous rattrapez de
l'eau chaud, si le feu n'evanouie pas et le *backdoor*—la
porte de derrière—n'est pas ouverte et le vent ne siffle
pas trop forte. . . .

CELESTE: Ah oui, Monsieur, c'est bien simple!

* * * * * * *

ASTONISHMENT

One of the most astounding scenes in the local
panorama of human oddity is a news-stand at one of
the big terminals when the homeward-bound commut-
ers are buying their evening papers. Those who be-
lieve there is no hustle in New York might contem-
plate that spectacle—the continual patter of hurried
people scampering up to the counter to seize a paper,
throw down their money, and bound away. Indeed, if
you stand for a while near the news-stand and watch,
you will gradually become aware that there is something
pathologic about the matter; that the great mass of
newspaper readers crave and swallow their daily potion
much as they would a familiar drug or anodyne. The
absolute definiteness of the traffic is another curious
feature: the news dealer can tell you, almost to a figure,
how many of each paper he will sell each evening. As
the commuters hurry up to the counter, you will never
see them hesitate, ponder, and ask themselves, "Well,
which paper shall I read to-night?" No; they grab
the usual sheet, and off they go.

* * * * * * *

Maxims and Minims

We wrote* something about the spider's "struts and cantilevers," and were gently chaffed by some friendly correspondents. Well, the spider is not only a marvellous engineer, he also seems a persistent patriot. There is one on our front lawn who still celebrates the Spanish-American war. Every morning, among the sun-sparkled shrubbery, we find he has erected a dewey arch.

One of the most exciting things we know is a series of dainty models at the Natural History Museum in New York, showing the various stages in a spider's web. Did you know, for instance, that often a preliminary spiral is blocked in, to hold the web together during construction? This is afterward carefully removed to make room for the sticky spiral which does the fly-catching. So at any rate we remember the Museum's models. If you find being stricken with astonishments a pleasing humiliation, the Museum is the place to visit. We always think to ourself, how old Sir Kenelm Digby would have enjoyed it.

Then, of course, you mustn't omit to read Fabre's glorious *Life of the Spider*. The microscopic Archimedes can much more than mere tenuous trusses and gossamer girders. M. Fabre tells us that the triumph of the spider's unconscious art (for the creature works divinely, without reason or calculation) is the logarithmic spiral. So if by chance you have ever fallen into that meanest absurdity of the unthinking and

---

*You can refer, if you insist, to a book called *Plum Pudding*.

asserted that "Mathematics is uninteresting," consider
Fabre's words:—

Geometry, that is to say, the science of harmony in
space, presides over everything. We find it in the ar-
rangement of the scales of a fir-cone, as in the arrange-
ment of an Epeira's lime-snare; we find it in the spiral
of a Snail-shell, in the chaplet of a Spider's thread, as
in the orbit of a planet; it is everywhere, as perfect in
the world of atoms as in the world of immensities. And
this universal geometry tells us of a Universal Geo-
metrician, whose divine compass has measured all
things.

The mathematician, let us add for our own part, is
the greatest of poets, the greatest of priests.

But a study of M. Fabre's magnificent books will not
necessarily add consolations to the Pollyanna brand
of religious thought. You will find, in his discussion
of the appalling married life of insects, gruesome con-
siderations which will furnish merriment to the cynic
and painful grief to the old-fashioned. M. Maeter-
linck says, in his eloquent preface to *The Life of the
Spider:*

Nothing equals the marriage of the Green Grass-
hopper, of which I cannot speak here, for it is doubtful
whether even the Latin language possesses the words
needed to describe it as it should be described.

The fiercest realist yet produced by the younger
generations of Chicago and Greenwich Village is a mere
trifler compared to the immortal Fabre.

*   *   *   *   *   *   *

Maxims and Minims

We are rather startled to find, on beginning to read Edward Lear's immortal *Nonsense Books* to our Archurchin, that liquor plays a considerable rôle in his waggishness. This phase of Lear's works we had quite forgotten, although it may have played a subtle part in undermining our character when young. But what are we to do, we ask, when, in reading aloud we come upon such distressing testaments as this:

B was a Bottle blue,
which was not very small;
Papa he filled it full of beer,
And then he drank it all.

Or this:

There was an Old Man with an Owl,
Who continued to bother and howl;
He sat on a rail, and imbibed bitter ale,
Which refreshed that Old Man and his Owl.

Or this:

There was an old person of Sheen,
Whose expression was calm and serene;
He sate in the water, and drank bottled porter,
That placid old person of Sheen.

Now, of course, in reading these passages we can improvise variations: we can say that Papa's blue bottle was filled with tea; we can substitute "ginger ale" for "bitter ale"; we can make the old person of Sheen sit in the porter and drink bottled water; but before

[257]

The Powder of Sympathy

very long our audience will begin to read the book for himself, and when he finds that we have implanted a false version in his mind there will be a swift succession of logical inquiries. The Old Soak's problem is far easier: *his* sons are grown up and become "revenooers"; their minds were long since formed on this topic. But what is the comparatively Young Soak to do in the matter of explaining literature to his offspring?

Only in one place, as far as we can see, does Mr. Lear refer to drink with any tinge of moral or reprobatory feeling. Thus:

> Twas a tumbler full
>   Of Punch all hot and good;
> Papa he drank it up, when in
>   The middle of a wood.

We shall have to lean heavily upon that cautionary stanza in reading to the Urchin. We will not try to bias him, of course; but by grave and solemn repetition surely the idea will pierce his meninges—that no matter how excellent the libation, it must be performed in secret and far from scrutiny.

* * * * * * *

THE SEDAN

Not long ago, in the garage at Salamis run by our friend Fred Seaman, we were admiring and examining a very beautiful sedan. Not that we had any idea of ever abandoning our cherished Dame Quickly, who means more to us than any other vehicle ever will or can. But, just in a contemplative spirit, and as a

Maxims and Minims

frustrated lover of luxury, we were admiring this sedan, and saying to ourself that if we were a person of wealth and standing that would be just about the kind of car we would like to own. And we gazed entranced at its opulent upholstery, its cut-glass carnation-vase, its little 8-day clock, cigar-holder, and all the other gauds and trinkets. Just in idle curiosity we inquired the price. Then we went over the hill to our home.

A day or so later a cheerful Polish friend of ours, who is so kind as to call for the washing weekly, and who used to do odd jobs round our estate, and with whom we boarded our admirable cat *Pepys* while we were in town, called at our house. Titania had always represented this person to us as being in the last agony of financial dissolution and a worthy object of charity.

"I want to show you my new boat," said he.

We thought at first that he meant an actual boat, down in the harbour, and were interested. But he pointed out to the front of the house. There was the very sedan we had admired. He insisted on our going down to listen to the engine. "Paid all cash for it," he said proudly.

When we see a large, glimmering limousine pass us on the road, hereafter, we shall always wonder whether it is some thrifty washerman and his family.

*　*　*　*　*　*　*

BAD VERSE

Really thoroughly bad verse (as Mr. Hilaire Belloc pointed out in an essay) has a magic and an attraction all its own. It has (he said) "something of the poign-

The Powder of Sympathy

ant and removed from common experience which you get also in poetry. Great pits strike one with horror, as do the mountains with their sublimity."

A philosophic friend of ours, whose dolorous task it is to examine manuscripts for a large publishing house, sent us the other day a collection of verses that had been submitted to his firm. We have had considerable diversion in examining them; though compositions of this sort lead one also to melancholy. It is sad to think that the accident of rhyme, which has been the occasion of so much verbal loveliness, has also been responsible for so many atrocities.

We shall not say who wrote the verses in question, except that he lives in a Southern State, but we will quote a few stanzas from a poem called "Love's Progress." After several pages describing the sorrows of a pair of lovers, we arrive at this:

> They broke to break their breaking breach,
> Which both have caused, because of each
> Failing to procure, or reach,
> The longing goal they did beseech.

> They sought to seek their seeking truth,
> Which all do crave, and never boot;
> They kept their cadence to a flute,
> Which only wisdom seeks to mute.

> They slid to slide their sliding sleigh
> Toward goals, bu met a fray;
> And, striking, struck the striking broil;
> And found themselves to winds a spoil.

Maxims and Minims

They swung to swing their swinging life
To higher spheres and lusty fife;
But flung against the sturdy cliff,
And sunk beneath the brutal grief.

They shed their shedding tears in vain,
Fruitless as the dismal rain;
And pined their pine, and pined it more;
And reaped their crop they sowed to store.

Defying fies have they defied;
Lying lies have they belied;
Brisky thought did both deride;
Happy hope had both denied!

You see how low rhyme can bring a man.

Of the following, our friend the publisher's reader observes: "Alas, poor Henley—'twas an excellent fellow: I knew him well!"

I Am

I am the tutor of my mind;
I am the pastor of my soul;
All that pass, I leave behind,
And focus straight upon my goal.

Until we read that we felt sorry for the author; but indeed it takes him out of the sphere of charity.

TWO REVIEWS

I

(New York *Evening Post*, July, 1922)

IT IS curious that the agencies for letting people know about the things that really matter are so feeble and ineffective. There was published in England, last February, a book called *Disenchantment*, by C. E. Montague. It seems to us perhaps the first book we have seen that tells truth about the war, tells it beautifully, with a power and humour and tenderness that are palpable on every page. Five months have elapsed, and yet we have heard no word as to its being published over here. Worse still, we learn that more than one New York publisher, after reading the book, reluctantly declined it. Sometimes one fears that publishers are not unerring judges of what we all desire to read.

What does a man need to do to deserve well of his

Two Reviews

generation? Suppose he had written a book that with quiet dignity and restraint summed up the "ardours and endurances" of earth's greatest crisis; a book that showed sane and sweet knowledge of our poor, frail, tough, bedevilled human nature; a book so delicately and firmly written that the manner of it was no less potent than the matter; a book that dealt with furious subjects calmly; that reviewed passion and misery with reason and candour; a book that was bitter where bitterness was needed, but with the bitterness of antiseptic. C. E. Montague has written such a book. And even though it may be bad manners to speak about it publicly before it has been published here, we venture do so in the hope of speeding its coming. To confess a personal incident, when we were half way through it we encountered one of our friends who is a sagacious devourer of books. "What's worth reading?" he said. "Sit down at your desk and let me dictate a letter to you," we replied. With admirable docility this fine creature obeyed. We happened to know that he has an account at Brentano's, so we dictated thus: "Brentano's, New York. Gentlemen: Please order for me from Chatto & Windus, London, three copies of *Disenchantment*, by C. E. Montague, and charge to my account." We watched carefully while our friend signed his name, addressed and stamped the envelope, and dropped it down the chute.

By the time we had read him half a page of the book he had already decided to whom he would give his two extra copies. He will never regret the transaction, we swear.

The Powder of Sympathy

We are anxious to put a brake on ourself in speaking of this book: if we tried to tell you how deeply moving and true we found it, you might be alarmed. We admit that we came to it favourably prejudiced, for Mr. Montague's name has been honourable to us ever since we read his novel *The Morning's War*, published in 1913. We had heard, also, of his gallant record in the war: that in spite of his age (born in 1867), and an occupation (he is one of the editors of the Manchester *Guardian*) that many found a full excuse for non-combatancy, he enlisted as a private in 1914, rose through the ranks to a captain's commission, and was three times mentioned in dispatches. We also knew (from *Who's Who*) that his recreation was mountaineering, and that he had been awarded a medal "for saving life from drowning." But we found in this book so much more than we had imagined possible that we are at a loss to describe it. It is the kind of book that, like its author, "saves life from drowning." It may save some foundering reason from the dark tide of cynicism and disorder that is the natural result of the war years. Even if we only persuaded every newspaper man in America to read this book, we would have done a good stroke of achievement. It is a book peculiarly necessary for journalists to meditate.

It is very plain that the world to-day has a bad case of acid mouth, and Mr. Montague's book (to use a very humble metaphor) is a kind of litmus paper that shows the extent of our palate's embitterment. His reminiscent synopsis of the war's moods and its increasing disillusions and perplexities is the first account that

Two Reviews

seems to us to fit in with those troubled, enigmatic, and fragmentary confessions that one hears from those who saw the trouble from the under side; who are not always very articulate, but spasmodically ejaculate that "The war didn't get into the papers." The book deals with the greatest topic of our age in a spirit of commensurate greatness. Of course we think we can guess why some American publishers have been timid about it. In this country we have not been anywhere nearly so close to the war as Britain was. The war was still bullish with us when it suddenly ended. As a nation, we had not been in it long enough to feel that infernal douche of skepticism. England has been far, far more bitterly disillusioned. The war left us economically troubled, but spiritually much the same. The old bunkums, one suspects, still pass current here as they do not any longer in England. And perhaps this book, conceived in suffering and weariness, can be relished only by those who have been more deeply immersed in horror than most of us. Even in England, we hear, its sale has not been very large.

For, after all, humanity has an uncanny instinct to avoid truth as long as it can. As we read this book of Mr. Montague's we had a sudden vision of it selling as well as H. G. Wells does—passing from hand to hand, quoted, sermonized, becoming the fashionable topic of the season. It even made our beloved Santayana seem dim and pale, in a way; for it is so close and actual to our present moods and troubles. But then, with a sigh, we abandoned that vision. Why, if this book were really seized upon, gloried in as it deserves

[265]

to be, if its eloquent humour and generous brave spirit
were really acclaimed. . . . No, we can't quite see
it! The book is too beautiful, too true.

II

(New York *Herald*, October, 1922)

They don't come very often, the books that speak so
generously and beautifully to the inner certainties of
the mind. And when they do, it is desirable not to do
them dishonour by words too clumsy or sweeping.

But that Mr. Montague's *Disenchantment* has come
to us in just the way that it has is a curiously
mixed satisfaction and disappointment to the present
reviewer. Satisfaction, in that for the past several
years I have been saying to every publisher who was
going abroad: "Why the devil do you go only to Lon-
don and nowhere else? Are you aware that there are
very exciting centres of literary activity in Glasgow,
Edinburgh, Manchester, Birmingham—all sorts of
places outside London. Some day"(I kept saying to
publishers) "one of the great books will bob up a long
way from London. You might remember, for instance,
Stevenson and Barrie. Now when you are in England
why don't you go to call on Mr. Montague at the
Manchester *Guardian?* He'd know what was going on.
Very likely he could tell you of someone who was writ-
ing a fine book—someone London wouldn't know
about."

I take no particular credit for saying this: it was ob-
viousness itself to any one who had noticed Mr. Mon-

Two Reviews

tague's earlier books. But the publishers, with their stereotyped habit of calling on a few literary agents in London, and thinking they have then done their possible, paid no attention. One of the odd things about publishers is that they have so little adventurous spirit about spooring for the really fine stuff.

Well, the book, quietly written and published, turned out to be by Mr. Montague himself. Half a year went by, but we in America heard nothing about it. There are always wide and well-polished alleys for the transmission of information amusing or trivial. Comparatively unimportant news spins along the parquet floor, and a crash resounds like that of tenpins tumbling. But humanity, probably with a wise instinct, averts its ear from matters that require meditation. The American publishers, seriatim, had their look at the sheets of *Disenchantment*. All apparently agreed that it was magnificent, but with their cheery assumption of knowledge as to what we want to read opined that it was too British or too full of intricate allusion or too much about the war, of which we were asserted to be weary. Or that the British publisher was asking an unwarrantable price for it; that only a few readers here would appreciate it; that it would be impossible to come clear on the expense.

These are all sound, sagacious reasonings. The one thing our publisher friends did not realize was that it is by publishing, every now and then, a book of this sort that they save their souls. It is an honour to put such a book on one's list, even if it should prove presently unprofitable.

The Powder of Sympathy

Disenchantment is an enchanting book. It is an *Anatomy of Melancholy* in the exact sense. It is a spiritual history of the war: a penetrating, intellectual, richly allusive, wise, sober, and compassionate study of that slow process of disintegrating certainty that marked every mind capable of independent action. People who have never read it probably imagine that the *Anatomy of Melancholy* is a dismal and grievous work. It is, however, one of the most richly amusing of all books; and it is only fair to say (accepting the danger of being misconceived) that Mr. Montague's delicious humour makes *Disenchantment* one of the most witty of contemporary writings. For war, after all, is a human institution and subject to the complexity of all planetary matters. It has, in Mr. Robert Nichols's great phrase, its ardours and endurances; also its selfishnesses, stupidities, and laughters. It is not to be supposed that men who are pompous and silly and hilarious and craven in business, book reviewing, education and theology will be otherwise when they go to war.

So Mr. Montague, in anatomizing the melancholy that has fallen upon the world, employs, with perfect skill and perfect restraint, every shaft in the quiver of a literary artist. The old devil of herd-poison lingers among us yet: there will be some simple spirits who will think this book bitter, some who will think it blasphemous; some who will maintain that it plays into the hand of Apollyon (whose residence, they will probably insist, is somewhere along Unter den Linden). But there will also be some, and not few I think, who will see in this book the breadth and burning spirit of

[268]

Two Reviews

one who has long gone beyond the conception of war as a merely national matter; who looks upon it as a movement of tragedy among men where the innocent suffer no less outrage than the guilty. And yet even those who may find Mr. Montague's disrobing of official frailty almost too disturbing will take pleasure in the beauty of his text. Let no one prate to you of the luxuriant splendour of some of our accredited stylists. The deity of prose moves in Mr. Montague's pages. His savoury marrow of allusion—Shakespeare, for instance, has become part of his actual thinking tissue—will be undigested by some unpracticed readers. He will be, we might say, shrimp to the sundry; but no harm will ensue: the casual reader will merely pay Manchester compliment for what belongs first to Stratford. And Mr. Montague deserves all the compliment that is possible in an uncourtly world.

This book could only have been written by a man who has been through the scorching and weariness. Its simplicity, its calm, temperate understanding of human weakness, the optical vividness of its narrative passages, the generous sympathy that moulds even its ironies—these are the possession of experience. And it occurs to me to ponder the courage and fortitude of one who could sit down, in the sobriety of retrospect, to write a book recalling beauties and sufferings that most of us would have been glad to let slide into the discard of memory. There could have been only one motive, and only one sustaining power, potent enough to carry the hand through so bitter a task. A love of humanity and a generous hope of humanity's increase of sanely inno-

The Powder of Sympathy

cent happiness could beget a book as noble as this; no other emotion could avail.

And still the troubled reviewer feels—this being three months after his reading of the book, and no mere snapped off opinion—that he has not done justice to the subject. For this book is not merely one of the noblest passages of political writing that he knows of, and not merely one of the most clearly and beautifully moving exhibitions of honest thinking. It is a book that is sanative and antitoxic for the present time. He is a shallow observer indeed who does not see, in the post-bellum world, muddy currents of cynicism and discontent; revulsive twitchings, literature no less jangled than politics. Mr. Montague does not disenchant us from any enchantments that were worth keeping. Except the politicians and the ultra-parsonical parsons, we had slipped their leash long ago. He offers a lucid enlarging mirror of truth and sense in which a thoughtful reader may see enlarged and brightly snuffed the small sooty flame of his own natural candle, as William Penn called the inward spirit. He magics us for the moment by his charm and the lovely humanity of his vision into thinking that we, too, can, if we will, be just, liberal, and humane.

BUDDHA ON THE L

IN FRANK SHAY'S bookshop we found *A Budd-hist Catechism*, by Subhadra Bhikshu. We have never known much about the Buddha—so little, in fact, that we thought that was his name. (His name was Prince Siddhartha Gotama.) But we have always felt that he was a kinsprit.

We opened the book at random and the first thing we saw was:

95. *Did not the Buddha give us any information concerning the first beginning and ultimate destiny of the Universe?*

No;

The Powder of Sympathy

96. *Did he know nothing about it?*
   He knew, but he taught us nothing.

There was a subtlety about that that pleased us greatly. It reminded us of a Chinese mandarin of our acquaintance who says that the universe was Dictated but not Signed. Immediately we forked out $1.25 to Frank Shay and took the book. Frank was so pleased to sell a book (business is said to be at a very meagre pulse in Greenwich Village in midsummer) that he at once responded by buying our lunch. We retorted generously enough by buying a copy of Anatole France's *L'Ile des Pingouins*, which we have been hearing about for ten years or so. We were interested to note that our copy is the "Cent Quatre-Vingt-Sixième Edition." Considering the book was published only fourteen years ago, that seems good progress.

Coming back downtown on the L we went at Buddha hard and with great satisfaction. We learned that Buddha is not a name but means a state of mind, or Enlightenment. We learned the answers to the following questions:

129. *Why has the upright and just man often so much to suffer here on earth?*
130. *How is it that the wicked and unjust man often enjoys pleasures and honours?*
118. *What is a meritorious action?*
109. *Why is not a layman able to reach Nirvana?*

We can hear you clamouring to know the answers to these exciting questions; they are right here before us; but our duty is not to solve problems, only to propound them.

[272]

Buddha on the L

But you must get it clearly in your minds that the Buddha is not a God. The Buddhist Catechism expressly rejects "a personal God-Creator," and "distinctly denies the doctrine of a creation out of nothing. Everything owes its origin and development to its own inherent vitalism, or, what comes to the same, its own will to live." The Buddha was not a God, but "a man far superior to ordinary men, one of a series of self-enlightened sublime Buddhas, who appear at long intervals in the world, and are morally and spiritually so superior to erring, suffering mankind, that to the childlike conceptions of the multitude they appear as Gods or Messiahs."

This is all tremendously exciting and leads to many pure and thrilling speculations that are much too honourable to pursue here. They would get us into horrible trouble, we feel sure. Indeed we are not at all certain whether both Frank Shay and ourself are not already subject to possible legal duress for vending and discussing so dangerous a book. But a noble analogy occurs to us which we venture with humility. Charley Chaplin is a great comedian. But the simple-minded drama critics are not content to leave it at that. They will have it (although it is now *vieux jeu*) that he is really a Great Tragic Artist. And so the tradition will go down to posterity that he was a Secret Hamlet, an Edgar Poe in clown's trousers. Charley himself, finding that his intellectual disciples insist upon this, perhaps acquiesces in the idea. Only by doing so, he may feel, can he get his stuff across.

It is really very astonishing; at this moment our

The Powder of Sympathy

Employer brings in to us a letter he has had from a publisher, which begins:

Do you agree with me that there is a need for a book on the fundamentals of public opinion, for a book that will endeavor to define the new profession of public relations counsel, its scope and its functions and its relations specifically to the press and to the public generally?

A Public Relations Counsel, of course, is simply the post-war name for a Press Agent. But we mustn't be ribald. The press agent, if conscientious, may contribute a valuable function. We ourself have worked as a free-lance Press Agent for George Fox, Sir Thomas Browne, Herman Melville, Thoreau, Lao-Tse, Pearsall Smith, and various other people who have seemed to us to have the Right Idea. But one of the troubles is that there have been (and always will be) a lot of unauthorized Public Relations Counsels who get the ear of the crowd and limn upon the great canvas of the public a portrait of the Prophet which is very different from what that poor dreamer himself may have wished. Even the humblest of authors has frequently cursed the publisher's man who writes the copy for his book-jacket. If you want a really pregnant speculation, weigh in your mind how many Public Relations Counsels there have been in the world of religion, and how amazingly they have interpreted and toned down the simple dissolvents of the founders of their creeds.

C. E. Montague, in *Disenchantment*, puts it beautifully:

Buddha on the L

Ever since those disconcerting bombs [i. e., *the words of Christ*] were originally thrown courageous divines and laymen have been rushing in to pick them up and throw them away, combining as well as they could an air of respect for the thrower with tender care for the mental ease of congregations occupied generally in making money and occasionally in making war. Yet there they lie, miraculously permanent and disturbing, as if just thrown. Now and then one will go off, with seismic results, in the mind of some St. Francis or Tolstoy.

The Buddha, sitting under his Bo Tree (*ficus religiosa*—and it is fairly obvious why so many philosophers have chosen fig trees to sit under; a really lusty fig will bear, according to the New International Encyclopædia, three crops of fruit in a season, thus keeping the eremite well fed; and a fig, L. E. W. says, is what he doesn't give for the ideas of rival magi) is to us an enviable vision. We wonder how his meditations would have fared if there had been a telephone at the foot of the tree.

The only drawback, as far as we are concerned, to becoming a Buddhist is the vow to abstain from intoxicating liquors. In this respect the Western religions seem to us more liberal. We have meditated long and earnestly on the subject and still have never been able to understand why an occasional exhilarating drink should be contrary to any wise man's ethic. Indeed, if Nirvana (or Perfect Release from Struggle) is the object of life, we have seen it well attained by three or four juleps or Tom-and-Jerries. The lay Buddhist has to take five vows; the Bhikshus (or Brotherhood of

[275]

The Powder of Sympathy

the Elect) take ten. Some of these additional vows required of the Bhikshu are:

I vow and promise not to eat food at unseasonable times—that is, after the midday meal.
I vow and promise not to dance, sing light songs, frequent public amusements, and, in short, to avoid worldly dissipation of every kind.
I vow and promise not to wear any kind of ornament, nor to use any scents or perfumes, and, in short, to avoid whatever tends to vanity.
I promise and vow to give up the use of soft bedding and to sleep on a hard, low couch.

These, we admit, present some difficulties. Frequenting "public amusements" offers too many opportunities for quibble. In one sense every possible mingling with the world is a public amusement. If there is anything more amusing than a smoking car full of men or a Broadway pavement at lunch time we don't know what it could be. Sleeping on a hard, low couch is easy enough—we can sleep anywhere with equal satisfaction, even on the floor. The queer thing that we always notice about every kind of moral code is that, sooner or later, it begins to lose sight of the distinction between essentials and non-essentials. Such matters as intoxicating drink and public amusements should not be (for the Western philosopher) subject to prescriptive legislation. The individual may very rightly impose restraints upon himself in non-essential matters; but to lay them upon him from above is to stultify the whole purport of ethics—which, if we understand it, is to encourage and develop a worthy personal will. And the Buddhist Catechism recognizes this in a very potent phrase—"Every one of us must become his own redeemer."

But Buddhism seems to have a firm grasp on one very essential and valuable idea, which is comparatively rare among religions. Thus the Catechism:

> 43. *Does Buddhism teach its followers to hate, despise, or persecute non-believers?*
>
> Quite the reverse. It teaches us to love all men as brethren, without distinction of race, nationality, or creed; to respect the convictions of men of other beliefs, and to be careful to avoid all religious controversy. The Buddhist religion is imbued with the purest spirit of perfect toleration. Even where dominant, it has never oppressed or persecuted non-believers, and its success has never been attended with bloodshed. The true Buddhist does not feel hatred, but only pity and compassion for him who will not acknowledge or listen to the truth, to his own loss and injury only.

Of course, all forms of human attempt to unscrew the inscrutable are fascinating and full of interest. The Westerner, however, is a bit troubled when he finds "Love of life on earth" listed among the "ten fetters" which, according to the Buddha, prevent the soul from receiving full freedom and enlightenment. That seems, to our earth-bound and muddied conceptions, a shabby doctrine. Even the most timid tincture of good manners suggests that a life so exciting, so amusing, so painful, so perplexing, and so variously endowed with unearned beauty and amazement deserves at least a

[277]

courteous gratefulness on our part. Mr. C. E. Montague (if you will allow us to quote him once more), explains what we mean:

Among the mind's powers is one that comes of itself to many children and artists. It need not be lost, to the end of his days, by any one who has ever had it. This is the power of taking delight in a thing, or rather in anything, everything, not as a means to some other end, but just because it is what it is. . . . A child in the full health of his mind will put his hand flat on the summer turf, feel it, and give a little shiver of private glee at the elastic firmness of the globe. He is not thinking how well it will do for some game or to feed sheep upon. . . . No matter what the things may be, no matter what they are good or no good for, there they are, each with a thrilling unique look and feel of its own, like a face; the iron astringently cool under its paint, the painted wood familiarly warmer, the clod crumbling enchantingly down in the hands, with its little dry smell of the sun and of hot nettles; each common thing a personality marked by delicious differences.

It is this sensuous cheerfulness in mere living, apparently, that the Buddhist would have us cast away. You remember Rupert Brooke's fine poem *The Great Lover*. Western students may be pardoned for wondering whether "Love of life on earth," whatever that life's miseries, ills, and absurdities, is not too precious to be tossed lightly aside.

INTELLECTUALS AND ROUGHNECKS

I

WE LOOK forward with keen interest to reading *Civilization in the United States*, the work of thirty-three independent observers commenting upon various phases of the American scene. So far we have only glanced into it, and have already found much that looks as though it needed contradiction. It is obviously going to be a gloomy book, rather strongly flavoured with intellectual ammonia. Of course, it is a healthy thing that some of our Intellectuals are so depressed about America. It is a good thing for a nation, as it is for an individual, occasionally to go home at night cursing itself for being a boob, a numbskull, and a mental flounder. But we feel about some of our Extreme Intellectuals as we do about the Physical Culture res-

The Powder of Sympathy

taurants. The people in these restaurants eat nothing but vitamines and plasms and protose; they live in an atmosphere of carefully planned Scandinavian hygiene; yet most of them look mysteriously pallid. And some of our most Conscientious Brows, in spite of leading lives of carefully regulated meditation, don't seem any too robust in the region of the wits.

However, we shall study this book with care. It contains articles by a number of people whom we admire specially. What we have been wondering is whether among its rather acid comments it gives any panoramic picture of the America we see daily and admire—an America which, in spite of comical simplicities and tragic misdirections of energy, seems to us, in vitality, curiosity, and surprising beauty, the most thrilling experiment of the human race.

In one article in this book we find the following:

> Everything in our society tends to check the growth of the spirit and to shatter the confidence of the individual in himself. Considered with reference to its higher manifestations, life itself has been thus far, in modern America, a failure. Of this the failure of our literature is merely emblematic. Mr. Mencken, who shares this belief, urges that the only hope of a change for the better lies in the development of a native aristocracy that will stand between the writer and the public, supporting him, appreciating him, forming as it were a *cordon sanitaire* between the individual and the mob.

Well, our confidence in ourself is not yet wholly shattered, in spite of the grinding horror of American

Intellectuals and Roughnecks

life. We feel confident enough to venture that this theory is dubious. Greatness in literature does not need to be protected from the insanitary infection of the mob. How Charles Dickens would have roared at such a timid little bluesock doctrine! Great writers do not need any clique of private appreciators or supporters. They are not produced by plaintive patter about ideals and the pride of the "artist." They arise haphazard, and they carry in them an anger, an energy, and a fecundity that deny all classroom rules. And the mob, heaven help us! is the ground and source of their strength and their happiness. Nothing can "check the growth of their spirit," because the spirit is big enough to turn everything to its own inscrutable account. You might as well say that Shakespeare couldn't write great plays because the typewriter hadn't been invented.

Of course, if by "a native aristocracy that will stand between the writer and the public," we are to understand an efficient service of tactful office boys and mendacious telephone girls to keep the chance caller from cutting the mortal artery of Time, we applaud. But we fear that is not meant.

When we get weary of upstage comments about literature we go aloft and have a talk to the fellows in the composing room (who, by the way, are all reading *Moby Dick* nowadays). There is no priggishness in their criticism. They have the sound, sober, sincere instinct—as when one of them tells us, with magnificent insight, that *Moby Dick* is "Hamlet stuff." When professional connoisseurs can teach us as much as the

composing room can about the human values that lie
behind literature, then we will mend our manners.

The more we think about it, the more we are stag-
gered by the statement that American life "tends to
check the growth of the spirit." To us the exact op-
posite seems true. American life as we see it all round
us seems to be crying aloud for a spirit great enough
to grasp and express it. It seems the most prodigious
and stimulating material that any writer ever had for
his contemplation. It is a perpetual challenge to the
imagination—a challenge that hardly any one since
Whitman has been great enough, or daring enough, to
deal with; but to say that it stunts the spirit can only be
valid as a personal opinion. It is to say that a hungry
man going into a restaurant loses his appetite.

II

We have ventured a little further into *Civilization
in the United States* (which someone has said should
really be called "Civilization between Fourteenth
Street and Washington Square") and, to tell the truth,
we are astounded. This time we are astounded by the
extraordinary mellow gravity of the Young Intel-
lectual. It is sad, by the way, that the editor of the
volume is actually not much younger than ourself; but
indeed he makes us feel immeasurably aged and de-
cadent.

There are, of course, admirable things in the book.
Mr. Mencken is at his best in his attack upon Con-
gressional mediocrity. Messrs. Macy, Van Loon,
Lardner, and Ernest Boyd carry us with them, as they

Intellectuals and Roughnecks

very often do. Mr. Henry Longan Stuart's "As an Englishman Sees It" is the most quietly pregnant of the essays we have read. But we must confess that when the editor (Mr. Harold Stearns) writes on "The Intellectual Life" he leaves us puzzled and unhappy.

Perhaps Professor Colby's contribution on "Humour" affords a clue. At first we did not quite "get" it; we did not realize that Mr. Colby was having his little joke at the expense of some of the masculine Hermiones who met fortnightly (so Mr. Stearns assures us) at the editor's home "to clarify their individual fields, and contribute towards the advance of intellectual life in America." After reading the appalling solemnities of Mr. Stearns's Preface we realize how charmingly Mr. Colby is (as becomes a veteran) chaffing the young pyrophags. He remarks that the "upper literary class" in America is utterly devoid of humour. This intramural stab he must have meditated at one of those fortnightly meetings while the chairman was remarking that "the most moving and pathetic fact in the social life of America to-day is emotional and æsthetic starvation."

When young men of thirty or so begin to talk about "contributing to the advance of intellectual life in America" they should do it with a smile. Otherwise someone else will have to do the smiling for them.

Consider the weight of the Great Problems faced by the editor of *Civilization in America* at those fortnightly meetings, while (let us hope) the elder members, such as Jack Macy and Professor Colby, smiled a trifle wanly—

[283]

The Powder of Sympathy

. . . "These larger points of policy were de-
cided by common agreement or, on occasion, by
majority vote, and to the end I settled no important
question without consultation with as many members
of the group as I could approach within the limited time
we had agreed to have this volume in the hands of
the publisher. But with the extension of the scope of
the book, the negotiations with the publisher, and the
mass of complexities and details that are inevitable in
so difficult an enterprise, the authority to decide specific
questions and the usual editorial powers were delegated
as a matter of convenience to me, aided by a committee
of three."

But you must read that Preface entire, to get the full
humour of the matter, to get the self-destroying serious-
ness of the Young Intellectual. It ought to be reprinted
as a pamphlet for the warning of college students.
Consider the syntax of the first sentence quoted above,
as a "contribution to intellectual life in America."
For our own part, after reading that Preface we couldn't
help turning to the quiet and modest little prefaces of
some of the great books, e. g., *Leviathan* and *Religio
Medici*.

We must not be ill humoured. The editor of the
volume, we are told, has made his own contribution to
the intellectual life in America by leaving for Paris as
soon as the proofs were corrected. He is perhaps a
victim of that oldest of American sophomore supersti-
tions—the idea that Paris is the only city of the world
where men of letters may enjoy true freedom of the
body and the spirit. Mr. Stearns has for some time
been threatening that the sterility and coarseness of

Intellectuals and Roughnecks

American life will drive our sensitive young men over-
seas. Well, the rest of us must shuffle along as best we
can, and see what we can do with this poor tawdry
civilization of ours. And incidentally, as a gesture of
divorce from American crassness, going to Paris and
taking a job on the Parisian edition of the New York
Herald seems to us inadequate. We are reminded of
another Young Intellectual—in Chicago this time—
who greatly yearned to write a masterpiece of obscenity,
but could not spell Messalina correctly.

Mr. Stearns speaks of himself and his friends as "un-
happy intellectuals educated beyond our environment."
There is a roaring risibility in this that leaves us
prostrate. The tragedy is that they apparently mean
it. We admire their sincerity, their high-mindedness,
and all that, but even at the risk of seeming argumenta-
tive we cannot, as long as honesty and clear thinking
mean anything, let that sort of remark go by unpro-
tested. It is impossible for any man to be educated
beyond his environment—whatever that environment
may be. For no man can be greater than Life itself,
and in whatever field of life he may be placed, if he has
the true insight and the true humility, he will find ma-
terial for his art. The extraordinary panorama of
American life, whatever its cruelties and absurdities,
should be glowing material for any artist with the
genuine receptive and creative gift. The real "artist"
(since our Intellectuals love that term) will not timidly
crawl into a corner and squeak; nor need he run away to
some imagined Utopia abroad.

Perhaps this is a more serious matter than we had

[285]

The Powder of Sympathy

supposed. We are one of the stoutest—one of the sin-
cerest, let us say, to avoid misunderstanding—partisans
of the Young Intellectual. We used to like, in our
wilder moments, to think ourself almost one of them.
But it looks now as though we should have to organize
a new clique—the Young Roughnecks. The Young
Intellectuals are too easily pleased with themselves.
In the first place, we honestly believe that few men have
any real critical balance and judgment before they are
forty. In the second place, the Young Intellectuals are
perilously devoid of humour. Of that rich, magical,
grotesque, and savoury quality they have far too little.
They have it, but it works spasmodically.

We welcome a book like *Civilization in America*
because it shows in a clear cross-cutting what is wrong
with a great many excellent young minds. They are
quick to scoff, but they are not humorous; they are
eager for human perfection, but want to escape from
humanity itself. They say a great many admirable
things, true things; but so condescendingly that, by
some quaint perversion, they impel us to fly to the op-
posite view. Life itself, apparently, is too multitu-
dinous, too terrible for them. They enjoy pouring
ridicule upon the world of business and upon the busi-
ness man. We should like to see them tackle their own
tasks with the same devotion and lack of parade that
the business man shows. Some of the most amazing
beauties of American life have been the work of quiet
business men who were not clamouring for admiration
as "artists." Our friends the Intellectuals keep shouting
that the "creative class" (so they call themselves) must

Intellectuals and Roughnecks

be more admired, more respected, more appreciated. We answer, they are already respected and applauded as much as—perhaps more than—is good for them. Let them cease to consider themselves a class above and apart. They are too painfully conscious of being "artists." They make us feel like gathering a group of Young Roughnecks—let us say Heywood Broun and H. I. Phillips for a nucleus—and going off in a corner to be constructively and creatively vulgar.

THE FUN OF WRITING

O N THE way to the station this $\left.{\text{warm} \atop \text{chilly}}\right\}$ morning
[*Note to Linotype Man: Please kill the inappropriate adjective; we like to be accurate, and this April weather is so inconstant*] we were thinking how little appreciated is the true pleasure of writing.

Writing is an art (or, if you prefer, a trade) never wholly and properly enjoyed except by the intensely indolent. What we mean is this: there are a lot of things in life that are not at all as they should be. But the writer, by magnificent pretence, improves all that. Gardening, for instance. No one enjoys seeing beds thickly decorated with bright flowers and superb vegetables more than we do. But the grubby and tiresome task of groping about with trowels and quicklime and all the other fertilizers is distasteful. Getting sweet peas to climb is a noxious business. Somehow the seedsman always palms off on us a kind of horizontal sweet pea that runs lowly along the ground and

The Fun of Writing

never blossoms at all.   But take up the pen, or type-
writer, and how quickly everything is rectified.   When
you set to work to compose a story, how easy it is to
have things nice and genteel.   Thus:

Out in the bland freshness of the suburban morning,
Mr. Frogbones was enjoying his garden.   In twin beds
under the tall French windows the gardenias and sun-
flowers were just opening towards the violent orb.
Sweet peas and daffodils and vast claret-coloured roses
aspired upon a green trellis.   "How I love a little nose-
gay," he said, as he clipped off a couple of dozen of the
great cider-tinted chrysanthemums, and bore them in-
doors to his wife.   In the breakfast room a well-trained
maid servant was putting the fragant coffee on the
table and the children were drinking their morning
milk with neatness and gusto.   "Elise," said Mrs.
Frogbones to the maid, "you may bring in the sausages,
kidneys, bacon, scrambled eggs, anchovy toast, marma-
lade, grape fruit, porridge, raisin bread, and gooseberry
jam.   Mr. Frogbones is ready for breakfast."

Now what could be easier, what could be more agree-
able, than to write that?   And yet not a word of it is
true.   We know Henry Frogbones well: his garden is
contemptible; the maid's coffee is execrable, and she
is going to leave at the end of the week anyway; his
children roar with anguish when they see a mug of
milk, which they detest.   But how pleasant it is to
lend a hand to the travailing universe when you are
writing.

As Henry Frogbones finished his ample breakfast the
large absinthe-coloured limousine rolled with a quiet

The Powder of Sympathy

crunch across the terrace which was pebbled with small blue gravel. He slipped on his new herringbone surtout, lit a fine black cheroot, hitched up one spat which had got twisted, and rolled away to town. Ambrose, the chauffeur, was accustomed to his employer's ways: he drove gently so that Mr. Frogbones could read the morning paper with comfort. After an hour's ride through exquisite scenery [*if the editor pays more than five cents a word, it may be well to describe this scenery*] Mr. Frogbones reached his office, where the morning mail had already been opened and classified by a competent assistant. In the anteroom a number of callers were waiting, held in check by a respectful young man who was explaining to them that no one can possibly disturb Mr. Frogbones until his morning article is written. . . .

As a matter of fact, we don't feel that we can go on with this any further; it is beginning to seem too unlikely. But it only seems unlikely to us, because we know the truth about old Frogbones. The average magazine reader would swallow it without cavil. That is why we say that writing is huge fun, because you can solve all the perplexities and distractions of life as you go along, and really enjoy yourself at the same time, and (most remarkable of all) get paid for it.

A CHRISTMAS SOLILOQUY

I

IN THE most peaceful spot known to American life—
a railroad train—we had several hours of that pleasure which offices are devised to prevent, viz., meditation; or even (if we may dare so high) thought. Our thoughts, or whatever they are that go round inside you when you are sitting passively in a train, were tinged by the approach of Christmas.

There was evidently something in the bright air and pre-Christmas feeling of that December afternoon that even softened the heart of the news butcher, for we noticed as the train hastened along the Connecticut shore his manner became more and more fond. He began, at Grand Central, in a mood of formality, even austerity. "Lots of nice reading matter here, gentlemen," he cried. "Get a nice short story book" (by "book" he meant, of course, magazine) "to kill time for a coupla hours." We thought, perhaps a little

The Powder of Sympathy

sadly, of the irony of begging men to annul Time when they had happily reached almost the only place in America where it can be enjoyed, examined, taken apart, and looked at. But, perhaps due to a niggardly spirit among his congregation in the smoker, the agent gradually became more fraternal. His manner was almost bedside by the time we had got to New Rochelle. "Choclut pepmints, figs, and lemon drops, fellas!" And at Stamford he was beginning to despair. "Peanuts: they're delicious, boys." We made up our mind, by the way, as to the correct answer to our old question, Where does New England begin? The frontier is at South Norwalk, for there we saw a sign *The New England Cereal Company*. And just about there, also, begin the billboards urging Codfish, surely the authentic image and superscription of New England.

Of course there is a great deal to think about in the signs you see along the track. There is that notice:

> DANGEROUS
> LIVE WIRES
> KEEP AWAY

which is a good advice socially as well as electrically. But we thought that these warnings were a bit unfair to New England, where there are fewer human Live Wires than there are south of the Harlem Strait. We remembered a certain club in Philadelphia of which the bitter-minded used to say it was the only organization in the

A Christmas Soliloquy

world whose membership was 100 per cent. Live Wires, Regular Fellows, and Go-Getters.

As we went through Greenwich, Riverside, Westport, we admired the blue shore of Long Island lying so placidly across the Sound. And it struck us almost with a sense of shock that there are a great many people to whom Long Island is only a dim, unreal haze on the horizon. Yes, foreign travel is a brisk aperient to the mind. We remembered, as we always do when travelling on the New Haven, Robert Louis Stevenson's delight when he first went that way. In one of his letters he speaks of the succession of beautiful rocky coves that saluted his eye. "Why," he wrote, "have Americans been so unfair to their own country?"

It would be impossible to tell you all the things we thought about: they have already faded. We did not forget our duty, as a travelling mandarin, to be a little magisterial when occasion seemed to require it. In the station at New Haven, for instance, there is a young woman, most remarkably coifed, who presides at the tobacco counter. She seemed of a notably cheerful and lenient disposition, and we ventured a remark upon the weather. She said she wished it would snow, so that she could have some real fun, by which she meant, we dare say, a little bobsledding with the youths of Yale College. We thought that this showed a dangerous inappreciation of her general opulent good fortune in being young, comely, and attached to a tobacco traffic. We looked at her quite sternly and said, "Young women can always have a good time, no matter

The Powder of Sympathy

what the weather." To our regret, as we hastened on toward the Springfield train, we heard her squeaking with mirth.

But the starting point of our meditation was an attempt to describe and dissect this curious pre-Christmas feeling, which is one of the most subtle and genuine adventures of the whole year. When we try to examine it in its components we see that the whole thing is too delicate and pervasive for analysis. What are its ingredients? we said to ourself. We thought of the little shrill tingling bells of the Salvation Army; we thought of the warm juicy smell of roasting chicken that outgushes from a certain rotisserie in Jamaica, Long Island. We thought of the bright colours and toys in the windows of that glorious main street in Jamaica, which is where we do our Christmas shopping. We thought of all the sparkle, the chill, clear air, the general bustle of the streets, that one associates with the Christmas season; and of the undercurrent of dumb and troubled realization of human misery and stupidity and frustration that comes to some more clearly now than at any other time. And we thought also of the mockers and the cheerful skeptics, to whom any candid expression of a simple human emotion is cause for nipping laughter. Never mind, we said to ourself, there is at least one time of year when they can all afford to put away their shining paradoxes and their gingerbread cynicisms —like the gilded circus wagons we saw shut up in winter quarters at Bridgeport.

Probably the most sensitive and complex of human sensations is the pre-Christmas feeling: because it is

A Christmas Soliloquy

not merely personal but communal; not merely communal but national; not merely national but even international. We know then that for a few weeks a great part of the world is busily thinking of the same things: how it can surprise its friends, how it can encourage the miserable, how it can amuse the harmless. Even the dingiest street has its pathetic badges of colour. It is a great thing to have such a widespread community of sentiment, which, however varying in expression, is identical in essence. One may be amused when he sees the Christmas Annuals published by Australian magazines and finds under the title *A Happy Christmas in New South Wales* a photograph of girls in muslin enjoying themselves by picnicking along shady streams with canoes and mosquito nettings. That kind of Christmas, we think, would seem very grotesque for us, but our friends the New South Welsh evidently find it exhilarating.

But it is that mysterious and agreeable pre-Christmas feeling which is the best of the whole matter. Christmas Day itself is sometimes almost too feverish a business of picking up blizzards of wrapping paper, convincing the Urchin that his own toys are just as interesting as the Urchiness's, and treading on tiptoe for fear of walking on the clockwork train or the lurking doll. At Christmas time we always think—probably we are the only person who does—of the late admirable William Stubbs, once Bishop of Oxford and Regius Professor of history, the author of those three fat mulberry coloured volumes *The Constitutional History of England*, a work far from easy to read, and which,

The Powder of Sympathy

when we were compelled to study it, seemed of an intolerable dullness. Bishop Stubbs, in the dreadful words of the *Dictionary of National Biography*, "never forgot that he was a clergyman." It is also said that "his lectures never attracted a large audience." But what we are getting at is this, that on Christmas Day, 1873, the excellent Bishop retired from the gambols and gayeties of his five sons and one daughter and wrote the preface to his History. We love to think of him, worthy man, shutting himself up from the Yuletide riot in roomy old Kettel Hall (now a part of Trinity College, Oxford) and sitting down to write those words, "The History of Institutions cannot be mastered —can scarcely be approached—without an effort." Now that we are somewhat matured, we think that we could probably reread his *Constitutional History* with much profit. In that Christmas Day preface, written while the young Stubbses were (we suppose) filling the house with juvenile clamour, there is one phrase that catches our eye as we take the book down for its annual dusting:

"Constitutional History reads the exploits and characters of men by a different light from that shed by the false glare of arms. The world's heroes are no heroes to it."

II

We shall remember the Christmas of 1921, partly, at any rate, by the wonderful succession of pellucid, frosty, moonlit nights that preceded it. We walked round and round our rustic grange trying to focus just

A Christmas Soliloquy

what we wanted to say to our friends as a Christmas greeting. A curious misery was upon our spirit, for we felt that in many ways we had been recreant to the spirit of friendship. When we think, for instance, of the unanswered letters. . . . We have sinned horribly. Yet we wanted to give ourself the selfish pleasure of saying a word of affection to those who have been kind to us, and to whom, in the foolish but unavoidable hurry of daily affairs, we have been discourteous. (The way to love humanity, we said to ourself, is not to see too much of it.) Moreover, to write a kind of Christmas sermon is, apparently, to put one's self into the loathsome false position of seeming to assume those virtues one praises.

We remember the first clergyman who made an impression upon our childish mind. It was in a country church in a village where we were visiting some kinsmen. This parson was a great bearded fellow, long since gone the way of flesh. He was a bit of a ritualist; his white surplice and embroidered streamers of red and gold impressed us enormously. He came very close to our idea of Divinity itself. We used to sit and hear him booming away and think, vaguely, how wonderful to be as virtuous as that. When the organ throbbed and his vast gray beard rose ecstatically above his white-robed chest we thought that here was Goodness incarnate. Years later we asked what had become of him. We heard that he had lost his job because he drank too much. The more we think about that the tenderer our feeling is towards his memory. Only the sinner has a right to preach.

[297]

The Powder of Sympathy

Thinking about this pre-Christmas feeling, and wanting to say something about it, but not knowing how, we got (as we started to tell you) on a train. We went, for a few hours, to another city. There we saw, exhilaratingly different, but fundamentally the same, the shining business of life going forward. The people in that city were carrying on their own affairs, were hotfoot upon their own concerns; we saw their eager, absorbed faces, and what struck us was, here are all these people, whose lives are totally sundered from our own, but they have, at heart, the same hopes and aspirations, the same follies, weaknesses, disgusts, and bitternesses as ourself. And the same would be so of a thousand cities, and of a hundred thousand. Then we got into one of those things called a sleeper, which ought to be called a thinker. An ideal cloister for meditation. All down the dark aisle we could hear the innocent snores of our fellows, but we ourself lay wakeful. We felt rather like the mystic Russian peasant who goes to bed in his coffin. We were whirled along through a midnight landscape of transparent white moonlight, and, quite as cheerful as the dead child in Hans Andersen borne through starry space by the angel, we made our peace with everything. We claim no credit for this. We would have slept if we could. There was a huge bump in the middle of the berth, and there was a vile cold draught. We read part of Stephen Crane's magnificent sketch *The Scotch Express*. But those miserable little dim lamps——

And then, strangely enough, there came a sudden

A Christmas Soliloquy

realization of the amazing richness and fecundity of life. Every signboard along the railroad track is an illustration of it. Hideous enough, still it is a kind of endless vista into the huge jumble of human affairs. Here is a billboard crying out something about a Spark Plug, or about the Hotel Theresa; or on the side of a little shabby brick tenement a painted legend about Bromo Seltzer. Someone worked to put that advertisement up; someone had sufficient credulity or gambling audacity to pay for it; somewhere children are fed and clothed by that spark plug. Christmas itself suddenly seemed a kind of spark plug that ignites the gases and vapours of selfishness and distrust and explodes them away. Everything seemed extraordinarily gallant and exciting. Take the Hotel Theresa, for instance. We had never heard of it before. It is on 125th Street, we gathered. We would like to wager that all sorts of adventures are lying in wait up there, if we can slip away and go looking for them.

As we were lying in our cool tomb (Carl Sandburg's phrase) in the thinking car, we meditated something like this: Christmas is certainly a time when a reasonable man should overhaul his religion and see if it amounts to anything. Christmas is a time when millions of people are thinking of the same thing. Humanity is so constituted that you can never get the world to agree about things that have happened; but it is happily at one about something that probably never happened—the Christmas story as told in the Gospels. If millions of simple people believe a thing,

The Powder of Sympathy

that doesn't make it true; but perhaps it makes it
better than true: it makes it Poetry, it makes it Beauty.
Stephen Graham says, in that moving book *With
Russian Pilgrims to Jerusalem* (which certainly ought
to be read by every one who is at all interested in re-
ligion; it is published by Thomas Nelson & Sons; you
may have to get it from London, we don't believe it is
in print over here)—Stephen Graham says:

True Religion takes its rise out of Mystery, and not
out of Miracle.

Religion, which has proved to be one of the greatest
dividing and hostilizing forces in the world, is in its
essence just the opposite. Surely, in the origin of the
word, religion means a binding together, a ligament.
Now take the most opposite people you can think of—
say Babe Ruth and the Sultan of Turkey (is there still
a Sultan?); or say Mr. Balfour and the chap who runs
the elevator in this office. No matter how different
these may be in training and outlook, there will be
some province of human thought and emotion, some
small, sensitive spot of the mind, in which they can
meet and feel at one. We can imagine them sitting
down together for lunch and having a mutually im-
proving time, each admiring and enjoying the other.
Widen the incongruity of the individuals as much as
you like: imagine Mr. Joseph Conrad and Dr. Berthold
Baer; or Mr. James W. Elliott (the Business Builder)
and Mahatma Gandhi—we care not who they are, if
they can make their thoughts intelligible to each other

A Christmas Soliloquy

they can find that remote but definite point of tangency where any experienced mind can meet and sympathize with any other human mind, discussing the problems of destiny which are common to all. It is this Common Multiple of humanity, this sensitive pulse in the mind, this realization of a universal share in an over-burdening mystery too real to be ignored, but too terrific to be defined or blurbed about, that is the province of religion.

And then the devil of it (for there is always a Devil in every sensible religion) is that the best way to be sure there is this possible point of junction is not to attempt to find it. Both Mr. Balfour and the cheerful elevator boy would probably pray heartily to be delivered from sitting down to lunch together. This mysterious mental sensitive spot that we speak of remains sensitive only as long as it remains private and secret. Perhaps religion can be defined as a sense of human fellowship that is best preserved by not being too companionable.

We were thinking, too, how extremely modern and contemporary the Christmas story seems. It is appropriate that the final instalment of the Income Tax falls just before Christmas. The same thing happened 1921 years ago. "There went out a decree that all the world should be taxed," says Luke. That was why Joseph and Mary went to Bethlehem—to pay their tax. And we can imagine that the Bethlehem *Evening Star*, if there had been newspapers at that time, would have had a column of social notes just similar in spirit to those of our own press to-day. The arrival of Jo-

The Powder of Sympathy

seph and Mary would not have been noticed. We
might have read:

Mr. and Mrs. Pharisee of "White Sepulchre," Gali-
lee, are spending the winter at the Tiberius Hotel.

The Hon. Pontius Pilate, Governor of Judæa, is en-
joying a week-end visit with Tetrarch and Mrs. Herod
at the tetrarchal mansion.

Mr. and Mrs. Philip Herod are travelling in Syria for
the winter. Mrs. Herod was before her marriage Miss
Herodias, socially prominent.

Prof. Melchior, Prof. Balthazar, and Prof. Gaspar
arrived last night from the West. They are said to be
in town for some astronomical investigations. The
professors had great trouble in securing hotel accommo-
dations, the city being so crowded.

Rev. Caiaphas, one of the most respected High Priests
in this diocese, has an apartment for the winter at
Philactery Court.

The train pursued its steady way through the moon-
light, and the silvered loveliness of earth and trees
made us think generously of our own country. We
are still foolish enough to love this America of ours with
a dumb queer love. We still believe that in spite of
Senates and Live Wires, in spite of the antics of some
of the half-educated and well-meaning men who "gov-
ern" us, this country has a unique contribution to make
to the world in future years. There should be inter-
national Christmas cards: there should be some way
of one nation surprising another with a friendly mes-
sage on the Morning of Mornings. We believe (per-
haps we are not impartial) that the English-speaking

A Christmas Soliloquy

race, by its contributions to human liberty, has a right to a leading place in the world's affairs; but if it gives way to its characteristic vice of arrogance, we weary of it. We think of the feminine brilliance, charm, and emotional volatility of France; of the beautiful sensibility and self-control of Japan; of the melancholy idealism of Russia; of the sober industry of Germany. Have we, then, nothing to learn from these? Printers' ink is scattered about these days with such profusion that it becomes almost meaningless. Sitting in the subway, and raising our eye plaintively from a newspaper to an advertising card, we have wondered which was the greater menace, Pyorrhea or Japan? Both were said to be menaces. It is our own conviction that nothing can be a menace to America but itself.

This seems a dismal kind of Christmas homily, but we enjoyed ourself immensely while we were meditating it in our lower berth. Very likely if it had been an upper berth the result would have been different. In any case, we take the liberty of wishing our friends —who are, by this time, too indurated to feel surprise or chagrin at anything we may say—a Merry Christmas. We wish for them a cheerful and laborious New Year, with good books to read, and both the time and the inclination to think. We even wish for them occasional eccentric seizures, such as we feel at the present; when we have a dim suspicion that behind the noble and never sufficiently praised comedy of life there lies some simple satisfying answer to many gropings. A simple thing, but too terrible and far-reaching ever

The Powder of Sympathy

to be wholly put into practice by puzzled and compromising mankind. We mean, of course, the teachings of Christ. Consider the German generals and military men, who lost everything. But the German toymakers conquered the world.

THE END

www.ingramcontent.com/pod-product-compliance
Lightning Source LLC
Chambersburg PA
CBHW030516100426
42813CB00001B/69